Cross-Cultural Adoption

Cross-Cultural Adoption

How to Answer Questions from Family, Friends, and Community

Amy Coughlin and Caryn Abramowitz

LifeLine Press
An imprint of Regnery Publishing, Inc. • Washington, D.C.

ISBN 978-1-62157-186-5

The Library of Congress has cataloged the hardcover edition as follows:

Coughlin, Amy.
Cross-cultural adoption : how to answer questions from family, friends, and community / Amy Coughlin and Caryn Abramowitz. p. cm.
ISBN 0-89526-092-1
1. Intercountry adoption—United States. 2. Interracial adoption—United States. I. Abramowitz, Caryn. II. Title.
HV875.55.C69 2004
362.734'0973—dc22

2004012771

Published in the United States by
LifeLine Press
An imprint of Regnery Publishing, Inc.
One Massachusetts Avenue NW
Washington, DC 20001
www.Regnery.com

Distributed to the trade by
Perseus Distribution
250 West 57th Street
New York, NY 10107

Interior photographs by Dave Ritz

Manufactured in the United States of America

10 9 8 7 6 5 4 3 2 1

To all the people in governments and private agencies, both near and far, who work tirelessly to bridge continents and help create families.

And to Dad, whose precious gifts to me—kindness, playful wisdom, and a quiet, unconditional devotion—I hope to pass on to my own children. — A.C.

Contents

Foreword by Rocky Bleier ix

Introduction xi

1. The Questions Kids Ask

What does "adopted" mean? 5

Where is she from? 7

Why did they go all the way over there to adopt a child? 9

Who are her "real" parents? 11

Why didn't her "real" parents want her? 13

Was she abandoned? 15

Why does she look different? 17

Is she my real cousin? 19

Where was she before she was adopted? 21

Why didn't they just have one of their own? 23

Why are there so many little girls, and not as many boys? 25

Did she have a different name when she was born? 27

How much did they pay for her? 29

Will she be able to understand me and speak English? 31

What if they want to give her back? 33

What if she wants to leave them and go back to her birth parents? 35

Will she remember where she was born or who her birth parents were? 37

Won't she feel sad when she finds out she's adopted? 39

2. Do's and Don'ts for Grown-Ups

Do's

Do treat her like any other kid 45
Do support her when curious strangers ask questions 46
Do respect her privacy 48
Do treat prospective adoptive parents the same as expectant parents 49
Do acknowledge and celebrate the differences 50

Don'ts

Don't introduce her as adopted 53
Don't say how "lucky" she is 55
Don't assume adoption is a second choice 56
Don't jump to conclusions about the birth mother 57
Don't tell us we're sure to have "our own" now 58

3. Want to Know More about Her Birth Country?

The People's Republic of China 65
Russia 77
The Republic of Guatemala 85
The Republic of Korea (a.k.a. South Korea) 93
The Republic of Kazakhstan 101
Ukraine 107
The Republic of India 115
Socialist Republic of Vietnam 123
The Republic of Colombia 133
The Republic of Haiti 141

Appendix: Resources for Learning More about Adoption 149
Acknowledgments 153
Index 155

Foreword

When my wife and I decided to adopt our two little girls from the Ukraine, we went through all the emotions, concerns, anticipation, trepidations and fear that all adoptive parents go through. We were petrified: we had so much to learn! Throughout that period, all of our focus was on us and the process, our responsibilities, on doing the right thing, on the health of the babies, getting the paperwork done, learning about adoption, and educating ourselves on the Ukrainian culture. The rest of the world temporarily did not exist for us, and that included our extended family. They were supportive but not necessarily involved. And they certainly weren't learning everything that we were learning about adoption and multi-cultural families.

This unique little book serves an important purpose. It helps that learning process. What it holds between its covers are some common-sense answers to some mighty big questions, especially for kids who have no idea that what they are saying may be hurtful, and for adults who don't necessarily know the right words when it comes to cross-cultural adoption. This is a great resource for extended family members and friends who are left out of the process and may not have the time or resources—but yet still have the need—to learn about cross-cultural adoption.

Common sense: two little words that mean so much, yet two little words that are so easy to lose sight of. Common sense is as simple as focusing on your surroundings with empathy for your fellow man. And common sense is what Amy Coughlin and Caryn Abramowitz offer in their book.

I came to know Amy and Caryn not through my sports career, but through something I hold even closer to my heart—my two daughters from the Ukraine. These two authors and I have something monumental in common: the amazing experience of adopting children from other countries. They have given me this opportunity to tell you what their book has to offer. I can sum it up in two invaluable words, which is pretty good for an old ballplayer who now makes his living speaking around the country. The two words are: common sense.

Rocky Bleier
Pittsburgh, Pennsylvania
May, 2004

Introduction

Two happy parents bring their adopted daughter home from China. A beautiful three-year-old girl, Lily is full of laughter and curiosity.

Her parents waited more than a year to adopt her. In that time, they learned about the issues involved in raising a child of a different race from their own. They learned that Lily might not bond with her new parents immediately, that she will likely go through a period of mourning at the loss of her homeland and caretakers—the only world she has ever known—and that she will be frightened, even of them, in the beginning. They also learned to prepare themselves for the questions that their families, friends, and strangers will ask about Lily and where she came from.

At the first big family gathering after Lily's arrival, six-year-old cousin Daniel is told to sit next to his cousin Lily at the table.

"But she's not my *real* cousin! She's *Chinese*!" Daniel announces triumphantly, obviously proud of his ability to understand the principles of biology and geography.

The room grows silent.

Daniel's parents, aghast at his innocent but painful remark, gamely try to explain to him that Lily is, in fact, his real cousin, that just because she's adopted, of a different race, and from another country, doesn't mean she's any less a real part of the family.

But the damage is done. Even though Lily is only three years old and still learning English, her crestfallen face is evidence that she understands the gist of what Daniel said: she doesn't belong. In that fragile period of bonding, Lily retreats into grief and confusion. A certain line of trust has been broken. Lily's parents scoop her up in the biggest hugs they can wrap around her, but she's unresponsive and remains subdued for the rest of the meal.

Daniel's parents apologize. "We meant to explain things to Danny and the girls, but we've just been so crazy busy lately. . . ."

This story is real. And even though it happened two years ago, the story is still painful for Lily's parents to retell.

In America today, the family unit is becoming the new, scaled-down model for the "great melting pot." Of the more than two million adopted children in the United States (not counting adult adoptees), 17 percent—nearly four hundred thousand—were adopted into cross-cultural families. While both cross-border adoptions and domestic transracial adoptions are on the rise, international adoptions, in particular, have skyrocketed, increasing by more than 300 percent since 1992. In fact, more than one in ten children adopted by Americans were born in another country.

Because adoptions—particularly international, cross-cultural, and transracial—are more common than ever, steady acceptance of cross-cultural adoptive families has spread across America. Those of us with adopted children who look nothing like us expect a certain loss of privacy and the host of questions and comments that go along with it, from strangers and family members alike. We have prepared ourselves for this extra attention, even if we are normally very private people, and have recognized how the use of positive adoption language can go a long way toward protecting our children's dignity and self-esteem and shifting people's sometimes faulty assumptions about adoption. But we are still often amazed at the number and breadth of questions our families generate.

Young children between the ages of four to seven, in particular, want to know everything about their new little adopted relative or friend. In their quest to understand how the world works, young children ask direct questions about adoption, with no implied judgments or hidden social meaning, and they want honest answers. "Who are her *real* parents? Where is she from?" And it is most often not the adoptive parents to whom these children direct their questions, but to their *own* parents or caregivers or teachers. If adults aren't careful, the answers can have devastating effects. Although an adoption is cause for joy and celebration (just like any time a child joins a family), scratch the surface a little and the backstory of each adoption is often spring-loaded with painful images of loss, desperation, oppression, and illness.

It's a lot for a kid with a healthy curiosity to handle.

A young child's first understanding of adoption can lead to irrevocably damaging remarks—or can lay a solid foundation for a developing wisdom about love, families, and relationships. It is often the adopted child's beloved young cousin or friend who, by one simple, ill-placed remark, unintentionally delivers the cruelest blow to the adopted child's sense of identity and belonging. The words people choose when talking about adoption matter very much. Positive adoption language shows respect and compassion for birth parents, adoptive parents, adopted children, and even for the children's birth countries and cultures. This book is a tool to help adults foster that respect and compassion by answering children's questions about cross-cultural adoption *before* everyone is gathered around the dinner table.

We are two adoptive mothers. When each of us, along with our spouses, decided to adopt a child from another culture, we joined the tens of thousands of prospective adoptive parents across the country who begin the emotional journey toward adoption every year. In the adoption process, which sometimes lasts as long as two years, we were counseled and educated about a smorgasbord of issues on raising adopted children. We listened, read, discussed, laughed, and cried in anxious anticipation of the wonderful event. With all this information, we were fortified.

We searched for a way to help our friends and families understand and share in celebration of our new cross-cultural families. Although there are a few resources available for families and friends of adoptive parents, including Pat Johnston's well-regarded book *Adoption Is a Family Affair*, we realized that the realities of modern life for most people we know—with their fully scheduled workdays and weekends, juggling of children's activities, and constant prioritizing of multiple tasks—left them with little time to dive into some of the longer and more complex books on adoption or attend workshops sponsored by adoption and family organizations. What we wanted was a handbook of easy reference that provides simple answers to complex questions, for those situations when simple answers are called for.

Simple answers to complex questions are never the whole story, of course, and not always appropriate in every situation. Just like anything that involves parenting and family relationships, adoption presents a mosaic of intricate issues, particularly if it involves a child who has suffered from neglect or abuse. Scholarly explorations of these issues can be found in your local library and bookstore, on the Internet, in workshops produced by adoption professionals, and in college and university programs across the country. Our aim in this book, however, is to provide answers to questions about cross-cultural adoption using positive, kid-friendly adoption language in a quick, question-and-answer format that is designed specifically for busy families.

The actual answers are far more complicated and divergent. There are a multitude of political, social, economic, and personal reasons why so many children are available for adoption. There are also a variety of reasons why people choose to adopt children from different countries and cultures. Each nation, parent, and child carries her own unique and complex story. Our intent is simply to introduce the concept of cross-cultural adoption in a way that promotes respect and kindness.

So this book is for all of you busy sisters and brothers, aunts and uncles, parents and grandparents, caregivers, friends, and teachers. It is not divided into narrative chapters, but instead into three separate sections. The first, entitled "The Questions Kids Ask," is a set of questions about international and other cross-cultural adoption that are often asked by young children. The questions anticipate issues and concerns that, if left unspoken or unanswered, could lead to unnecessary and long-lasting misunderstanding about the nature of family relationships. By posing the questions, we hope to identify for parents and caregivers subjects that might otherwise be neglected. The answers are honest but not detailed beyond a young child's comprehension, nor are they intrusive upon an adopted child's privacy.

We've framed the responses in ways that minimize harm to an adopted child's sense of identity and worth, while at the same time satisfying the curiosity of the child asking the question. Of course, there is no one right answer to any of these questions. And how much each child understands these issues varies with the age and personality of the child. You know your children best.

The second section, "Do's and Don'ts for Grown-Ups," offers tips for adults themselves—basic do's and don'ts that shed light on certain assumptions about adoption, infertility, birth parents, and the emotional experience of creating a cross-cultural family. Finally, "Want to Know More About Her Birth Country?" helps family and friends learn about and celebrate the cultures of the countries where these cherished children are born.

Our daughters are from China, a country where most of the children available for adoption are girls. For the sake of readability, throughout this book we have chosen to refer to the adopted child as a "she." We also have included the question, "Why are there so many little girls and not as many boys?" because we have been asked that question many times. Although many of the questions cross all borders and differences, not every question will apply to each family's circumstances.

Like most adopted children of a different race from their parents, each of our daughters will come to understand that Mom and Dad did not give birth to her in the traditional sense. Each will explore her identity in her own way. And, for better or worse, part of that identity is that they are permanent members of a community of family and friends whose inherent nature is to love each other unconditionally, even if we sometimes say the wrong things.

1

The Questions Kids Ask

This section is designed to help parents and caregivers teach their children about the sensitive, and often complicated, issue of cross-cultural adoption. It uses language and concepts that are easy for children to understand, but unlike a children's book, it puts the power of information where kids seek it most—in the mouths of their parents and caregivers.

In response to eighteen questions that children frequently ask about an adopted or soon-to-be-adopted relative or friend, we have provided two-part answers. The first answer ("For the young child") is designed for the ways that small children process information. As anyone who has spent time with a child knows, young children ask direct questions, want concrete answers, understand concepts in their literal meanings, and stop listening after their question is answered—which is usually after the first one or two sentences. Thus, each answer "for the young child" is purposefully short and has three objectives in mind: (1) to introduce positive adoption language and concepts during the crucial period during which young children are first forming their understanding of familial relationships; (2) to cultivate respect and kindness toward other children and other families; and (3) to reinforce the notion that families formed by adoption are no different than families formed by birth. If the answers appear to sugar-coat the realities of what can often be painful images of loss and abandonment, it's because these are words for little ears. A more sophisticated understanding of the world, with all its beauty and heartache, can come later. All true knowledge begins with compassion.

A few of the answers are also designed to gently remind children that some things about families are private and not open to discussion. Also, because young children who are learning about adoption are also just beginning to understand their *own* family relationships, some of the adoption concepts may cause a child to question the permanency and nature of his own relationships with parents and siblings. Therefore, many of the answers affirm the indestructibility of the questioning child's family bonds.

For the older child, who may understand more about the world and whose questions may demand a more complex or nuanced response, we have included a second and longer part to each answer ("Additional information for the older child or adult"). These longer responses have the same three objectives as do the answers for young children. We hope they will help form, at least in small part, building blocks for the countless bridges that connect our beautiful and imperfect cross-cultural society.

What does "adopted" mean?

For the young child:

Adoption is one way of making a family. Families are made in many different ways. Most times, to have a child, a mom and a dad get together and make a baby. Another way that a child joins a family is through adoption. That means the child grew in one woman's belly but another family raises the child. The child is "adopted" by the family. A child can be adopted at any age—from a newborn baby to a teenager!

Lots of people are adopted, and every family is different. Some families have one parent, and some have two. Some children are raised by grandparents or step-parents. What makes people a family is that they love and care for each other.

Additional information for the older child or adult:

The people in a family don't necessarily look like each other or act like each other. And the people in a family don't have to be related by blood—remember, a husband and a wife are not related by blood. Family members can be from different countries and different parts of the world, but no matter what they look like or where they come from, they belong with each other. The people in a family care about who each family member is deep inside, not just on the outside.

There are people whose job it is to help families and children come together so that the parents can adopt the child. These people are called adoption professionals, and they work for the government or for organizations called adoption agencies. There are official procedures that adoptive families go through to make the adoption legal and permanent.

A family can adopt one child or they can adopt a whole lot of kids. The love between a parent and a child—however that child came to be part of that family—is very strong and powerful, and it lasts forever.

Where is she from?

For the young child:

She comes from another country called ________ (e.g., Russia). It's far from here, all the way around the world. The people there are just like us—they live in houses, go to work, go shopping, cook dinner together, love their children, adore their grandparents, play games, and like to have fun.

Additional information for the older child or adult:

Now that she has been adopted by an American family, she is both ________ (e.g., Russian) and American. In fact, now her whole family, including her grandparents and cousins and aunts and uncles, has changed from Irish American to Irish and Russian American (or Chinese or African or Guatemalan, etc.).

It would be nice if we could learn more about where she comes from—what the land looks like there, what people eat, how they dress, and what their holidays and traditions are. It will teach us more about our world and is a good way to show her that we're interested in where she comes from. We can look on a map or a globe to see where her birth country is; we can read books and stories about her birth country; and we can search on the Internet for interesting facts and information. Her parents are very proud of where she is from, and we should be too.

It's important to remember also that she is American just like you and me. She's not alone in having come from another country. At some point, *all* Americans arrived from another country, either themselves or their parents, grandparents, or great-grandparents. Our family originally came from Germany (for example), so we are German Americans. When we got here, we made America our country. And as soon as her parents adopted her and she became their daughter, she also became American. Because she is going to grow up and live in America, and is part of a family, she will probably feel more American than she does _____ (e.g., Russian). She may not remember the place where she was born, and she may one day want to learn about it, just like many people who enjoy tracing their roots. Her heritage is an important part of who she is, just like our heritage is an important part of who we are.

More important than where she is from, though, is where she is now, and that's here with us. After all, it isn't where we were born that makes us who we are; it's where we live, with the people who love us and care for us.

Why did they go all the way over there to adopt a child?

For the young child:

Sometimes people adopt children here in the United States and sometimes they go to other countries to do so. There are children all over the world who need homes and families. And there are people (called adoption professionals) and organizations (governmental organizations and adoption agencies) that help bring together children who need families and families who need children, no matter where in the world those families and children live. Wherever their child is, that's where they go to get her.

Additional information for the older child or adult:

People decide to adopt children from different countries for a lot of different reasons. Sometimes they have a real interest in the culture of a particular country; they may have traveled there—once or many times—or maintained friendships with people in that country, or even studied the language. Other times, adopting parents have family members with ties to that country—some of their relatives may live there now or may have been born there years ago. And, at different times, there are more children who need homes in certain countries than in other countries, and that also affects the parents' decision.

One of the reasons that America is so special is that throughout its history, people from all different cultures have come here to live. The bringing together of different cultures is a long and important part of this country's history. It's one of the guiding principles upon which America was founded, and it's one of the reasons that this country is great. Diversity—meaning people who are different—makes a country stronger because people bring with them different ways of doing things, different ways of solving problems, building machines and buildings, cooking food, wearing clothes, making music, writing, singing—almost everything! Then we can learn from everyone else and have a much richer culture.

When parents adopt children from another country or culture, they may just want to be a part of this great American tradition of enriching our communities by bringing different cultures together. So, there are a lot of reasons why parents decide to go far away to adopt a child, but no matter where they go, her home is with them.

Who are her “real” parents?

For the young child:

She has two sets of parents: her birth parents and her adoptive parents. They’re both real. We refer to the mom and dad who gave birth to her as her *birth parents*, not her “real parents” or “natural parents.” The parents who adopted her are every bit as real and natural as those who gave birth to her. They are her real parents by adoption. When you see how her parents talk to her, hug and kiss her, play with her, read her bedtime stories, keep her safe, and take care of her when she’s sick, you can tell those are her real parents. Those are her real parents and she is their real daughter.

Additional information for the older child or adult:

Parents, whether by birth or adoption, are the people who raise their child. Parents teach their kids everyday things like how to wash their hands or build a sand castle, and bigger things too—things that will help their kids decide how to live their own lives one day. In exchange, kids make their parents laugh.

Sometimes the adoptive parents know who the birth mom and dad are, but sometimes they don't. It's not unusual for the child not to know who her birth parents are, and it's neither a good thing nor a bad thing. She is a permanent and important part of her family, and her parents (and her brothers and sisters) love her a whole lot. They are very proud of the heritage of her birth parents, and they are very proud of how their family was formed.

If her parents do know who her birth parents are, when she becomes old enough, she can decide for herself whether she wants to find out more about her birth parents. After she grows up, she may decide to try to contact her birth parents to see what they are like. Or she may grow up and, given the choice, decide that she doesn't want to contact her birth parents. Either way, it is a very personal decision for her and her family.

Why didn't her "real" parents want her?

For the young child:

Her birth mother and father wanted her very much, but they were not able to take care of her. (Remember, we call them her "birth" parents. Her adoptive parents are her real parents too.) Parents' love for a child is stronger than their desire to keep the baby when they know that they can't take care of her. They placed her for adoption so that she could be safe and well cared for and have a better life.

Don't worry, you won't be placed for adoption. You have plenty of other family members who love you and will take care of you if your parents can't, for any reason. They'll make sure you go to school and the playground, and will take you to do all your favorite things, and they'll be there for you always.

Additional information for the older child or adult:

There are many reasons why parents are unable to raise a child, and the reasons vary from family to family and from country to country. Maybe the birth mother and father knew that they would not be able to provide all the care and attention a baby needs. Maybe they died. Maybe they didn't have a house or enough food to eat or any way to send their child to school. Or the birth mother or father may have been too young to be parents. Sometimes, a government tells a family how many children they can have, and if they have more than that, they have to place the child for adoption.

Whatever it was, it didn't have anything to do with what the child did. The only thing we know for sure is that her birth parents realized that they could not give their child the proper life that she needed to grow up to be healthy, happy, and safe. They loved their baby so much that they placed her for adoption so that the baby could be safe, and well cared for, and have a better life, because they knew that there would be other mommies and daddies who would love and care for their child and make her a part of their family. What a hard decision that must have been! When they did that, they performed the most difficult and purest act of love there is.

Was she abandoned?

For the young child:

No, she was definitely not abandoned. Or rejected. Or given away. Her birth parents loved and wanted her very much. They made sure to place their child in the right hands as soon as possible—hands that could help her and knew what to do, like a social worker, a police officer, a hospital, or a church. They knew that there were lots of families who would want to adopt her and love and care for her. They did everything they could to get their child to a good and safe place as soon as possible so she would be taken care of and adopted by a family who could give her a better life. Her birth parents may have realized that they could not raise their child, but they did not abandon her.

Additional information for the older child or adult:

"Abandoned" is not a word we like to use when speaking about people, especially children. In most cases, it is hard to know exactly what happened or why the birth parents decided that they could not take care of their child. All we know is that it was a difficult choice, often forced upon them by difficult circumstances. However it was made, their choice resulted in the child being a dearly loved member of her family here. There are thousands of children around the world without families, and many of those children do find their "forever" families through adoption. Those children somehow make it to people who can bring them together with the families who embrace them and are able to take care of them. In that sense, they are not abandoned. For every child whose bonds with her birth parents are broken, there are hundreds of people who want to help her and love her. It's just a matter of finding each other.

Why does she look different?

For the young child:

She looks different from her parents because she comes from somewhere else. But lots of families look different from each other, even when the children are not adopted. Besides, except for identical twins, everyone looks different. It's kind of nice to look different—the world would be a pretty boring place if everyone looked the same!

Additional information for the older child or adult:

Sometimes kids look a lot like their parents. "He has the same chin as his father!" we often hear. Or a grandmother. Or famous Uncle Kirk. Families pass on a lot of similarities through their genes. When kids are adopted, they don't share the same genes as their parents, so they often don't share the same features. But even when the children are not adopted, lots of families still look different from each other. Tall parents can have short children; red-haired parents can have brown-haired children. Every person is unique. Everybody's face is special and belongs only to that person.

People from certain parts of the world often share features that look alike. People from countries in Asia, like China and Korea, for example, usually have dark hair and dark eyes. People from colder climates generally have lighter skin, and people from sunnier and hotter climates generally have darker skin so they can adapt to spending more time in the sun. But lots of people who aren't Asian have dark hair and eyes too, and many people from sunny climates still have light-colored skin.

There are things that are both the same and different in the way people look. Our faces all have eyes, noses, and mouths, even though they all have different shapes. We all have ears that we use to hold up our sunglasses. We all have skin that protects us from the sun and weather. We all (or most of us) have hair, too, but everybody's hair looks different. Some people like to make their hair look *really* different! It's fun and interesting to have many kinds of people who look different. And no matter how different anyone looks, a smile means the same thing on everybody's face.

Because so many people in America were born in another country—or have parents who were born in other countries—our classrooms, playgrounds, shopping malls, city streets, and offices are filled with people who look different from each other on the outside. But always remember, how we look on the outside isn't nearly as important as who we are on the inside.

Is she my real cousin?

For the young child:

Absolutely. Just like she is their real daughter, she became your real cousin as soon as she was adopted, and she'll be your real cousin forever. She's just like all your other cousins.

Additional information for the older child or adult:

Cousins come in all different shapes and sizes and from all different places. She'll do all the same cousin things that you do: have sleepovers, go on beach vacations, come to birthday parties, and eat holiday dinners. We're very lucky and proud to have her in our family.

Even if she doesn't look like other members of the family because she didn't inherit her parents' genes, she will have other traits in common with our family. She may be really good at swimming like her mommy, or love rock music like her daddy, or love to eat Italian food like Grandma. The more time she spends with the family, the more traits she'll have in common with everybody. And just like the rest of our family, we won't even notice that she may look different. Our family becomes richer and more interesting by welcoming people from other cultures and places.

Being a cousin—whether by birth or adoption—is a special bond that will stay with you forever. It will help you stay close when you've grown up. If you're very lucky, the close bond of being a cousin will allow you to have a special place in each other's lives. It doesn't matter where she was born or who took care of her at first, now that she is part of our family, she is your cousin. In fact, many people who are close to one another through years of friendship often call each other, or refer to their children, as "cousins." They do that because even though they may not have a blood relationship, they are so close that they feel like family.

Where was she before she was adopted?

For the young child:

She was in an orphanage. It's a place where babies and children live until they are adopted. [Or: She was with a foster family. They're a temporary family who took care of the baby until she was adopted.]

Additional information for the older child or adult:

Some orphanages can be very nice places where the children are taken care of by nannies and nurses who love babies. Other orphanages are not very nice places; there may be too many children and not enough people to take care of them. Kids who don't get adopted live in the orphanage until they are old enough to live on their own. Sometimes the orphanages are run by the government, and sometimes they are run by private agencies. The United

States used to have orphanages for its children who needed families, but now the government mostly uses foster families.

If she was with a foster family, they gave her all the things she needed—toys, a crib, clothes, food—and they took good care of her, too, and gave her lots of love. She couldn't stay with them forever because the foster family's job was to take care of her just until another family was found to adopt her and take care of her for the rest of her life. When that happened, it might have been hard for her foster family to say goodbye, but they were happy because they knew that now she'd have a permanent home and a forever family.

Why didn't they just have one of their own?

For the young child:

We don't ask why parents have babies, or adopt babies, or why they don't have any babies at all. Sometimes they choose not to make a baby themselves. Sometimes they can't make a baby themselves. Sometimes, realizing how many children in the world have no families, they want to open their family to a child who needs a home. Other times, a single parent wants to adopt. That's a very private matter and it's just between the parents. But no matter what reason her parents had for choosing to adopt her, she *is* their own and she always will be.

Additional information for the older child or adult:

When parents are in the process of adopting a child, they are bursting with joy and happiness, just like when a baby is born. It is a time for celebration! They can't wait to bring their child home and settle her into her new family. And just like when a baby is born, there are things about the child that will be new and different to the parents, and things about the parents that will be new and different to the child. They will have to learn things about each other and adjust to their life together. This learning phase can be quite a happy time because the parents and child know that they are becoming part of each other's past, present, and future.

After the parents have adopted a child, they don't think of her as their "adopted" child. She is their child, period. Even parents who have both adopted and biological children don't feel any differently about their children. They love each one just as much as the others and care for them in just the same way. No matter how a child comes into a family, she becomes part of that family forever.

Some families have a whole bunch of kids—children by birth and also children by adoption from different countries around the world, like India, Vietnam, and Russia. Which ones are their own? They all are!

Why are there so many little girls, and not as many boys?

For the young child:

In most countries, just as many boys are adopted as girls. But some countries have rules about how big a family can be, and when parents have to choose between a boy and a girl, the tradition in that country is to keep the boy. They love their little girls. It's not something that they want to do, but it's something that they have to do.

Additional information for the older child or adult:

In some countries, life can be difficult from the start and boys are needed to help with the work—whether it's farming, making and selling things, or building things; some cultures think that boys are more capable of taking on these jobs. And in some cultures, boys carry on the family name and traditions and also are responsible for taking care of the parents when they get old. It's not like that here in America. Here and in many other countries, girls are considered just as capable as boys to help with any kind of work, to carry on the family name and traditions, and to take care of their parents when they get old.

In some countries they have rules about how big a family can be. They have those rules because the country is so crowded that they are afraid everyone will suffer if the population gets too big. When parents have a baby girl and their living conditions and culture make the boys more desirable, the baby girl is placed for adoption.

Whatever country parents choose to adopt from, they just want a child to become part of their family. They don't care whether the child is a boy or a girl.

Did she have a different name when she was born?

For the young child:

Her birth parents, foster parents, or caregivers may have named her something different when she was born. But, just like you, she was given the last name of her American parents as soon as she became part of their family, and her parents chose her first name. Sometimes they keep the name she had. In every culture, it is an honor for parents to choose their child's name.

Additional information for the older child or adult:

Her parents may have chosen a new first name for her or they may have kept the name she had. Sometimes it depends on how old she was when she joined her forever family—the longer she had a certain name, the more likely she will want to keep it. Many times adoptive parents will use part of their child's name as a middle name, so the child might be called Katie Meiling Smith or Michael Scott Vladimir Jones. If you think about it, though, our country is filled with people with different-sounding names.

In many Asian countries, like Korea and China, when names are written in English, they often have three parts, and the last name (called the surname) is first. The next two names are called "given" names. Given names are often descriptive of a child's personality or appearance. Children are often named after flowers, precious stones, and forces of nature. For example, a Vietnamese boy might be named Giang (meaning river) and a girl Lan (meaning orchid). The Chinese girl's name Lin Yao means "beautiful jade treasure."

In European countries like Russia and Bulgaria, and in South American countries like Colombia and Guatemala, the given name is first, just like in the United States. Given names are usually rooted in the country's language and represent family members or historical and religious figures. So Baby Natasha and Andrei might come from Russia, and Baby Mariposa and Emilio might come from South America.

People are proud of the country where their families, ancestors, or children are from, and the names they choose for their children often reflect that country. Parents choose names for so many reasons—everything from honoring another family member or important person in their lives to celebrating a particular culture to choosing a name for the way it sounds or the way it's written.

How much did they pay for her?

For the young child:

No one pays for a child. Just as your parents paid the doctors and hospital bills when you were born, the adoptive parents paid the adoption agencies and lawyers to do all the adoption work. To all parents, though, their children are priceless.

Additional information for the older child or adult:

When a child is born, lots of people get paid: the hospital where the child is born and the doctors, nurses, and midwives. When a child is adopted, parents often pay adoption agencies, government organizations, and lawyers. It is never legal for children to be bought and sold for adoption—that is wrong and it's why there are adoption professionals to make sure that all legal procedures are followed when parents adopt children. The cost is not for the *child* but to pay for the services of people who bring the child together with her forever family.

Will she be able to understand me and speak English?

For the young child:

Of course! She'll be able to understand you, and she'll be able to talk to you. If she is very young when she is adopted, she won't even be able to speak at first, and the first language she'll learn is English. If she's older, then she'll learn to speak English, and it won't take her very long.

Additional information for the older child or adult:

If she is very young and not yet speaking *any* language, she probably won't even know any words from the language of the place where she was born. If she's a little bit older when she's adopted and can already talk, she may not know English at first and may take some time to learn it, but over time she'll speak as well as any other American kid. It may take her a while because she's used to a different language with different sounds, but that won't last long. If she is old enough to speak in her original language, her parents might be able to have her speak both English and her first language. Wouldn't she be lucky to know two languages at such a young age! Maybe she can even teach you a few words of her first language.

In the meantime, even if she doesn't know the words we are saying or is confused by the sounds we make, we can help her to learn by talking to her and listening to her. And lots of times, we are able to make people understand what we are saying without even using words. Hugs mean the same things in all languages and so do smiles. And, most important, whether or not she knows the words, we can show her in all different ways that we love her and are happy to know her and to have her in our family/lives.

What if they want to give her back?

For the young child:

They'll never, ever want to give her back, just like your parents will never want to give you back to the hospital where you were born. When a family is formed, the love that runs between the parents and the children is stronger than anything, and it lasts forever. Even when kids don't behave, or don't listen to their parents or teachers, or think that they've done something wrong, their parents still love them like crazy. There is nothing that kids can do that will make their parents stop loving them. Adoption is forever.

Additional information for the older child or adult:

Parents usually think long and hard about their decision to have a child, whether they give birth to or adopt their children. They think about all the things in their lives that will change when a child joins the family. And after they think about all these things, that's when they decide to add a child to their family. Once they make that decision, they make a commitment to love and care for their child forever. Parents want their children more than they want anything else in the world. Sometimes parents wait a really long time for their children to come into their lives. Sometimes parents have to travel a long way and do a lot of work to be able to adopt a child. After all of the waiting and the work, they want their kids even more!

What if she wants to leave them and go back to her birth parents?

For the young child:

Just like Dorothy in *The Wizard of Oz,* probably every kid—at some point when they're upset or angry—has threatened to run away from home or wondered what it would be like to run away from home. Sometimes when they're angry, kids (and parents too) will say things that they don't mean, including that they wished they were in a different family. These thoughts and angry words, although they can be hurtful, are normal. When a child who was adopted says she wants to leave and go back to her birth parents, she's not doing anything different than any other kid. And she doesn't mean it any more than any other kid who threatens to run away or to never speak to her parents again. It's just another way of expressing emotions that make her angry or sad or upset. Her family knows, and she knows, that they are her forever family, and that she doesn't really mean it. So when a kid who was adopted says in anger that she wants to go and live with her birth parents, she doesn't mean it any more than another kid who threatens to run away and live with Grandma.

Additional information for the older child or adult:

But that doesn't mean that a child who was adopted doesn't have any curiosity about where she came from. When she gets older, she may be curious about her past. She may want to try and find out where she was from and visit the city or town where she was born. A lot of people search for their roots even if they haven't been adopted. We all have curiosity about where we are from or who our ancestors were. The level of interest varies from person to person and from time to time. If she gets older and she wants to find out more about her past, that doesn't mean that she's unhappy with her family or that she wants to leave her parents. It just means that she is curious and doing what she can to satisfy her interest. Dorothy and Toto teach us a valuable lesson: "There's no place like home."

Will she remember where she was born or who her birth parents were?

For the young child:

In most cases, she probably will not have any memories of who her birth parents were because she was so young when she came to join her family here. Memories about what happened or people we knew when we were very young don't last. So, unless she was adopted when she was older, she probably won't remember that part of her life any more than you remember being in a crib or learning to walk or saying your first words.

Additional information for the older child or adult:

That part of her life was important to her and will be a part of her in some way, just not in a way that she'll remember. Her parents may have been given some photographs or other mementos of her life before she came to live with them and they will share these mementos with her. That way, she'll have a little piece of the life she had before she joined her family.

If she was four or older when she was adopted, she may have some memories of the orphanage or the foster home or even her birth parents. Those memories will stay with her and help shape who she is and who she becomes, just like your earliest memories of people and places have stayed with you. She may remember the nannies or caregivers at the orphanage, or her foster mother or father, maybe someone in particular who took a special interest in her, or maybe someone who gave her a special treat for her birthday or a holiday. She might remember some of the other kids she played with as a baby. But whether she remembers a lot or a little or nothing at all, she is with her real forever family now.

Won't she feel sad when she finds out she's adopted?

For the young child:

There won't ever be one point when she finds out that she's adopted, because her parents have been telling her from the very beginning about the special way that she came to be a part of the family. She has always known that she was adopted. When she is old enough to understand what being adopted really means, she may feel a little bit sad, confused, angry, disinterested, or even a combination of all different emotions. She may have a lot of questions for her parents. Her parents will try their very best to answer her questions and to make sure that she understands what an important part of the family she is, how much she is loved, and how lucky we all feel to have her in our lives.

Additional information for the older child or adult:

The word "adoption" will always be familiar to her and the way she joined the family will never be a surprise that her parents spring on her. Yet, when she does reach an age when she can understand what it really means to be adopted, she likely will have a lot of questions for her parents, and for other people, too, including her cousins and friends. If she feels sad or confused, or if she has questions, it is very important that we are honest with her and that we don't do or say anything that will hurt her feelings. The most important thing that we can do is make sure that she knows that we love her very much. Over time, her questions may be answered and much of her confusion will go away. Her parents will tell her everything they know about the circumstances surrounding her adoption. They'll tell her all they know about her past and how she became such an important part of their family. They'll describe to her the country and the city or village where she came from. They'll tell her the story about the first time they met—how she smiled or cried or laughed, what she was wearing, who held her first, and how they melted when they first looked into her eyes. They'll tell her about their first days together, how they got to know each other, and they'll show her lots of photographs. They'll tell her how she acted around them, if she was playful or sad, shy or excited. How much she ate and how little she slept. They'll tell her about her plane ride home and how thrilled all of her new relatives were to meet her and welcome her into the family—and how proud they are to be her mother and father. They'll tell her how much love they have for her birth parents because they are a part of her.

After they tell her all of that, they'll answer any questions she has, as well as they can. They will do their best to help her to understand who she is, and where she is from.

2

Do's and Don'ts for Grown-Ups

Adoptive parents want to be "just parents"—to adore their children and see them through the normal rough and tumble of childhood, adolescence, and young adulthood. But no matter how much adoptive parents want to be treated like any other family on the block, their status as a multicultural, adoptive family usually sets them apart. It is not only children who are curious about the adoption, but adults as well. Because adults (particularly close family members and friends)

often want to show their unconditional love and support for the adopted child, they may be reluctant to give voice to their curiosity over the circumstances of her adoption, afraid that their questions may be interpreted as disloyalty. Or they may hold certain assumptions about cross-cultural adoption that, left undiscussed, can sometimes lead to implicit messages to the adopted child that do more harm than good.

These "Do's and Don'ts" identify some fundamental concepts about the emotional experience of creating a cross-cultural adoptive family. Recognizing that a list of "do's and don'ts" often has a tendency to sound like a lecture, we want to emphasize that these are suggestions based on collective personal experiences in the adoption community. They are meant simply to provide helpful information to the supportive family member or friend who may wonder what to do if, for example, when spending time with the adopted child at a playground or in a store, a stranger approaches and wants to know all about how that child came to be part of the family.

Just as there are many different parenting styles, there are many different ways that adoptive parents incorporate the issue of adoption into their family's everyday lives. These suggestions are intended only to open the lines of communication between adoptive parents and their family members and friends, so they can freely discuss issues specific to their particular families. Adoptive parents are usually happy to talk about their concerns, hopes, and expectations for their children, and they realize that not all issues of importance to the modern multicultural adoptive family are matters of common knowledge.

Adoptive parents ask a lot of their family and friends. We ask that you treat us the same, but also that you treat us differently. We ask you to learn about the things that are important to us, and take special care with our children. Protect them from other people's curious stares. Tread carefully with your words. Be positive. Be wise.

Whether we have the right to make such elaborate demands, all we're really asking of you is to indulge the age-old, overwhelming desire to express how much we love our children.

Do's

Do treat her like any other kid.

It may be difficult and take a long time for adopted children to feel like they belong within their extended families. Often, treating these children like they're "nothing special" can go a long way toward making them feel at home and comfortable within the group. Avoid the temptation to spoil her because she didn't have everything that the other kids had in the first months or years of her life. (Grandma and Grandpa, we're talking to you here.) That means the rules and privileges apply to everyone equally: just like her sisters, brothers, and cousins, she doesn't get a cookie until she finishes her dinner; it's lights out promptly after two (okay, maybe three) bedtime stories; "please" and "thank you" must be said; and "no" means "no." Garden-variety expressions of affection and gentle discipline help a child feel safe and loved.

In many cases, children are adopted at such a young age that their American family is all they have ever known, so they won't feel any different unless they are made to feel different. But for children who were adopted when they were older, it's even more important to stem the instinct to spoil because no kid ever wants to feel "different" or "singled out." For some of these children, it will take time to trust their parents and form lasting bonds with their family members. It is not unusual for children going through the transition into their forever family to rebuff playful hugs and warm words, or even to say and do things that appear mean and hurtful. Protecting themselves against the pain of loss and disappointment has become habitual. In most cases, time and family counseling work to break these habits. The most valuable gifts you can offer these children are patience, routine, and consistency—and most importantly, regular unexaggerated expressions of love and devotion.

Do support her when curious strangers ask questions.

"That's so *sad* that she was just abandoned like that! She's so cute! I can't imagine her mother would just leave her on the side of a road!"

That's what a woman said to my sixteen-year-old niece while she was holding our daughter in her arms at a local Little League game. I don't think the woman bothered to take note whether our daughter was old enough to understand what she said, and I'm sure she intended no harm.

When curious (and sometimes thoughtless) strangers ask questions or feel the need to comment on the circumstances of the adoption, do not let them lead you along into inappropriate territory. Instead, gently steer them back to more suitable small talk. Respond in a way that shifts the conversation to positive adoption language and lets the child know that you are on her side. Example: "'Abandoned' is not really a good way to put it. A lot of care and love goes into the adoption process in China. Her birth mother made sure she was safe. She was well cared for there, and she is healthy and happy now."

To further ease the reproach so quickly targeted to birth mothers, you can ask the person to put himself or herself in the birth mother's shoes: "We all can understand the feeling of being alone, without any help, not knowing where to turn. What would any of us do if we really faced those circumstances, especially right after giving birth?"

Of course, if you feel the stranger has no business at all inquiring into your private lives, you might have to cut the conversation off altogether. More often, though, your responses will be general, short expressions of your pride and affection for the adopted child.

It is a curious phenomenon about adoption that people ask personal questions they wouldn't dream of asking in other situations. This is particularly true when the adopted child has special needs (i.e., when she faces physical, emotional, mental, or medical challenges). "Did they know about that when they agreed to adopt her?" "I've *heard* about all those bait-and-switch stories with those adoption agencies over there!" "Will the agency help them pay for all the medical expenses she needs?" As unnerved as you may be to hear these kinds of questions, it is especially important for the dignity of the child to address them head-on, rather than to let them pass in silence. Adoptive parents try to prepare themselves for these questions, and you should too if you plan on spending time with the adopted child in group situations. Your answers (delivered with a calm, matter-of-fact smile, rather than with anger or impatience) should be as much a message to the child as they are a response to the person asking the question. Example: "She is exactly the child her parents dreamed about and wanted, and we all think she is just perfect."

Depending on your comfort level, you may choose to treat these encounters as an opportunity to educate and spread goodwill. The person usually does not intend the message sent by his remarks, and it is rare that any well-meaning individual will resist a nudge in a direction that shifts the conversation to a more positive note.

Do respect her privacy.

Keep in mind that just because the adopted child looks different from the rest of the family, that does not automatically give strangers the right to have all their personal questions answered.

"Do you know who her natural parents are?"

"Did she have problems bonding with the family?"

"Are they really sister and brother? I mean . . . *really?*"

"How much did it cost?"

Adopted children have the same need for and right to privacy as you do. They do not want their entire life story being told to any stranger who stops and asks. Until a child is old enough to decide for herself how much information about her background she is willing to share, you should respect her privacy and avoid telling her life story to anybody who asks. If she hears you discussing the intimate details of her origins and family life with a complete stranger, she will likely feel awkward and embarrassed. Just because they ask does not mean you have to tell them.

It is wise to prepare yourself ahead of time to respond to strangers' questions, because they often come up at unexpected times or times when you're in a hurry. An example of a polite, nonresponsive answer to any or all of these questions: "She's from Guatemala and she's our ____ (granddaughter, cousin, best little friend from down the block, etc.). Yes, they're really sister and brother. We're very proud of the way our family was formed and we wouldn't have it any other way. If you want to know more about international adoption, you can call me and I'd be happy to talk to you about it. The U.S. State Department also has great information on its website."

As for the "How much did she cost?" question, which always stuns a little bit, an appropriate answer is: "You don't pay for a child. You pay the adoption agency and the governments for their work in making the adoption go through. Just like you pay for the hospital's costs and expenses when you give birth."

And of course: "She's priceless."

Do treat prospective adoptive parents the same as expectant parents.

Adopting a child is as exciting for soon-to-be parents as being pregnant. Yet because adoption is not as common as a pregnancy and many people have unexpressed (or expressed!) biases about adoption due to their unfamiliarity with it, family, friends, and co-workers may feel reluctant to talk about an impending adoption, perhaps assuming that it is a delicate topic about which the adopting parents are sensitive. In fact, adopting parents are not usually sensitive about their big event. They feel the same way all expectant parents do—overjoyed, overwhelmed, nervous, impatient, and, most of all, excited. Don't be afraid to ask the adopting parents about these feelings and to discuss the adoption with the same sense of excitement and levity that you bring to a discussion about pregnancy and childbirth. It is not a secret and not a source of embarrassment or shame.

Yes, there may be attachment and bonding issues if the child being adopted is a toddler or older and has suffered from neglect or abuse in the early months or years of her life. Children have strong emotional defense mechanisms, and it is not uncommon for children to act out or even reject their adoptive parents, for fear of losing them, even as the children and parents become closer. These are issues that adoptive parents of toddlers or older children are well aware of (and for which there are numerous sources of support in the adoption community), but the potential for bonding and attachment problems neither lessens nor alters the parents' joy over their impending adoption. It is no different than expecting parents' worries over the potential for genetic or medical conditions in the baby about to be born—topics that nobody would dream of bringing up in the joyous anticipation before the baby's arrival. The bottom line is that a child is being brought into a family—a small miracle no matter how it occurs.

Do acknowledge and celebrate the differences.

Your young adopted relative or friend has an entire cultural ancestry that is probably different from your own. As she grows older, her sense of self will likely incorporate not only her here-and-now family and friends but also the history and traditions of her birth country. Each child will connect to her heritage in her own way and to a different degree than another. The only fact that will be common to virtually all adopted children in cross-cultural families is that their ethnicity cannot be ignored. Trying to ignore it, even with the noblest of intentions—"*We're all just American!*"—can often do more harm than good. It may make the adopted child feel ashamed of her heritage, that it—and, therefore, *she*—is not worthy of recognition or respect. It also may breed resentment and guilt over her developing desire to learn more about her background.

One of the best things you can do to show your support and love for the adopted child is to learn, even a little bit, about the history and culture of her birth country. Read a book or two. They don't have to be dry school texts; literature written by a native author or historical novels set in her country of birth provide fascinating insight and details into the area's culture and history. (See Part III for suggested literature from and about the top ten countries from which Americans adopted in 2003.) Another source of easily accessible and comprehensive information about a country is travel books. Even if you have no plans to travel there, there is no better way to get a feel for a country than by reading a crisply organized *Fodor's*, *Lonely Planet*, or *Let's Go* travel book. Demonstrating an understanding and celebration of another's culture is a sure sign of respect that has improved relationships everywhere from the kindergarten classroom to world summit conferences.

Don'ts

Don't introduce her as adopted.

Sounds pretty basic, right? Everybody knows that. It's used as a telltale sign of bad character in the movie *The Royal Tenenbaums*, released in 2001, to demonstrate the careless disregard of a father (played exquisitely by Gene Hackman) for the feelings of his family. "And this is my adopted daughter, Margot," he says when introducing Gwyneth Paltrow's character. He grins blithely and pats her shoulder as he says this, while Gwyneth cringes and retreats deeper into sullen despair.

In introductions, do not distinguish between adopted and non-adopted children. The pain this inflicts is obvious. The adopted child feels inferior, like she falls into a different category and will never be considered a real part of the family. The rule is simple: Don't ever, ever do this. Never.

Take note of how often adoption is improperly used as a label. In this modern world of information onslaught by newspapers, magazines, television, and the World Wide Web, feature and news stories all too often refer to people as being adopted when that fact is irrelevant to the story. "Police officers said the house belonged to the adopted son of the school superintendent." "Tom Cruise and Nicole Kidman continued their custody battle over their two adopted children." The use of the word "adopted" as an unnecessary identifier in the media passes by most people's eyes unnoticed, so familiar are they with the journalist's choice of words. But to adoptive families, that choice of words—inadvertent as it may be—repeatedly drives home the message to the public that people who were adopted must always be differentiated from those who were not, and that children who were adopted are somehow less genuine than those who were not.

Another concept adoptive families are working hard to change is the common use of the term "Adopt-a-" (fill in the blank) by companies and organizations for fund-raising activities. We have all encountered these campaigns a hundred times: Adopt-a-Whale, Adopt-a-Highway, Adopt-a-Tree. This is really just another way of asking people to contribute money toward the care and maintenance of an item or animal. Most adults can distinguish the short-term commitment of money to a worthy cause from the permanent commitment of parents to a child. But many children who are just learning about what adoption means may be confused by the term, especially because a good number of the "Adopt-a-" programs are targeted to children (particularly the popular "Adopt-an-Animal" zoo programs and the "Adopt-a-Book" library programs). These fund-raising gimmicks have led to playground taunts of adopted children, equating them with cases of charity or wild animals. Most companies and organizations have no idea of the implications these "Adopt-a-" programs have for children and their families, and when contacted by adoptive parents have immediately and graciously changed their slogans to the more appropriately titled "Sponsor-an-Animal" or "Gift-a-Book."

What may seem to some people harmless matters of semantics are to people touched by adoption issues that go to the heart of the sacred and everlasting familial bond of adoption.

Don't say how "lucky" she is.

How many times we adoptive parents have heard this:

"She's so *lucky*!"

"Such a *lucky* little girl to have you two as parents."

"What a generous thing you have done."

"If it wasn't for you, can you *imagine* the horrible life she would have had? What would have become of her?"

Hearing this enough times, the adopted child feels like a lifelong charity case, rather than the cherished daughter that she is.

Yes, she is lucky. So is any child who has a supportive, loving family. And we parents are lucky, too, to have been able to create this family: to hear this tiny beauty sing to herself in the morning, to feel the rush of devotion as two little hands are thrust out toward us for a hug, to laugh out loud at the squealing ball of high-spirited energy at the dinner table, her face covered in spaghetti.

Parents are not usually driven by selfless generosity or noble intentions when they choose to adopt. We simply want a family. And we feel lucky to have one. The "luck," therefore, is mutual and won each day through the same combination of love, compassion, respect, and good fortune that is at the heart of any "lucky" family.

Don't assume adoption is a second choice.

People build families in different ways and for different reasons. It is true that many parents choose adoption because of infertility, but it's also true that many choose adoption for other reasons, including personal beliefs and other medical or genetic conditions. A pitying look, a sad but courageous smile, helpful suggestions ("Have you tried *acupuncture*?"), and unsolicited comments about fertility treatment ("You're adopting? But I've heard the success rate for *in vitro* has gotten much better!") all share the same, possibly faulty, assumption: the adopting parents are biologically unable to have children and are settling for second best. But along the continuum of parenting decisions, "choices" are fluid concepts. Why did the parents choose to adopt? The answer may be a combination of things, the answer may keep changing, or you may never get to know the answer. Issues of fertility, arising as they do behind the closed doors of bedrooms and doctors' offices, are the most confidential of matters. With adoption rates in this country skyrocketing—research shows that one-third of the nation is touched by adoption within their families—it is unwise to assume that all those hundreds of thousands of parents chose to adopt only after exhausting fertility treatments.

The reasons people choose to adopt are as varied and unique as the people themselves. Mistaken assumptions, including the age-old, "Now watch, you'll be pregnant before you know it!" diminish the joy that should be the center of attention. Instead of celebrating the experience, and the hope it embraces, these remarks carry a negative message and judgment that, though unintended, is surely felt at some level. The degree to which people choose to discuss the reasons for adoption is highly personal and worthy of the same respect that is accorded the most private spheres of life. (Nobody ever asks "Why did you conceive?" or "Can you tell me the details of your artificial insemination?") Many people choose to adopt not because they are out of other options, but rather because they believe that adoption is the *best* option.

Don't jump to conclusions about the birth mother.

Mothers throughout the world who relinquish their children face immense criticism. Often thought of as weak, irresponsible, cheap, and worthless, they suffer a lifelong pain that is far greater than any that childbirth brings. Please don't jump to the wrong conclusion that these women are any different than you and me or that they love their children any less than we do. Enormous pressures—all too frequently stemming from the lack of paternal responsibility that unfortunately crosses all cultures and generations—often force them to do the unbearable. In many Asian cultures (and not long ago, in the United States as well), the stigma against single parenthood is more powerful than we can imagine. Single motherhood not only brings irrevocable shame to the mother, the child, and the extended family, it also violates fundamental concepts of Eastern religions grounded in family bonds and male-centered lineage. Adoption is not a choice for these women, not in the same sense that Americans—with our birthright of colossal freedoms—understand the word "choice." In many European, Asian, African, and South American countries, crushing poverty, unfair laws, civil wars that leave families without fathers and governments without order, and lack of access to birth control grind the mothers' options down to a terrifying trio: abort, try to take care of the baby amid overwhelming danger and despair, or relinquish the child for adoption. Adoptive parents are eternally grateful that these mothers had the courage to choose the latter.

Even if none of these external forces was a factor in the relinquishment decision, some birth mothers have the strength and honesty to realize that they are simply unable to properly care for their child. Perhaps these are the bravest women of all.

We adoptive parents often hear: "How could her mother *just leave* her?" Or: "They don't care about their children over there."

Nothing could be further from the truth. Reports and interviews with birth mothers show that these women universally live with unending sadness, grief, and guilt over the loss of their children. The increasing incidence in this country of open adoptions (i.e., adoptions in which the birth mother or father, or both, play a part in the adoptive family's lives) is doing a lot to alleviate that kind of suffering in domestic adoptions. But most cross-cultural adoptive families know little or nothing about the circumstances that led their child's birth mother to relinquish her child. The only things we know are that we love our children's birth mothers because they are a part of our children and it is because of them that our beloved children are who they are. And the only things we have to give them in exchange for the wonderful gift they gave us are what we hold in our hearts—respect, compassion, a prayer to ease their pain, and, of course, a promise to love our children as bravely as they do.

Don't tell us we're sure to have "our own" now.

She *is* our own. Believe it or not, those parents who chose adoption because of their infertility do not continue to secretly harbor lifelong yearnings for a biological child. Having "our own" now is irrelevant; the child we have is the one we want. It is inconceivable that we could love or want any child more.

Talk to any adoptive parents and they will tell you that no matter how many times they have heard this comment, they don't really know how to respond to the suggestions and judgments implicit in it. By regaling us with anecdotal stories of women who found themselves pregnant shortly after adopting, you are somehow demoting the wonderful thing that has just happened to us to a second-rate experience—as if she is just something to distract us until the "real" thing comes along or a means to a more desirable end. Certainly, we understand that such remarks are not intended to cause insult, confusion, or pain. And we are not so sensitive that we can't handle the comments or respond politely by explaining that the underlying assumption is not only invalid, it is misinformed and maybe a bit judgmental. The real problem is that rather than the focus being where it should be—on the family that is being formed and the love that is the foundation for the decision to adopt—the attention is shifted to other defensive-sounding explanations that diminish the adoption experience.

Love for a child is the most joyous feeling in the world. We cannot imagine, nor do we wish for, anything better than what we have right now. Like all parents, we have the best.

3

Want to Know More about Her Birth Country?

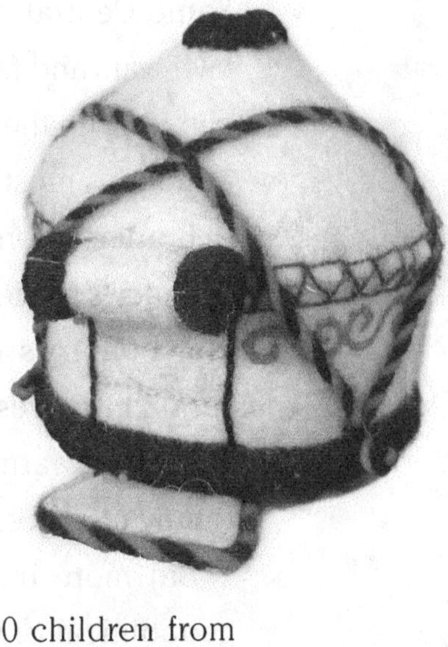

Wars, economic low tides, and government instabilities have driven the current of international adoptions over the past half-century. In his eloquent, research-packed book, *Adoption Nation: How the Adoption Revolution is Transforming America*, Adam Pertman explains that from 1948 to 1953, Americans adopted approximately 6,000 children from Germany, Greece, and other battle-scarred countries in Europe, along with nearly 2,500 Asian children, two-thirds of whom were Japanese. The aftermath of the Korean War in the 1950s and the Vietnam War in the 1970s brought huge numbers of orphaned children from those countries into the waiting arms of mostly white American families. As these countries regathered their political and economic strength, the rate of adoptions beyond their borders decreased.

A nation's economic health and stability often determines its capacity to keep biological families together. South Korea remained the leader in international adoption for decades until China (with the implementation of its one-child population control policy) and Russia (with the breakup of the Soviet Union and its concomitant social upheavals) opened their borders in the 1990s. Some Central American countries, struggling through civil wars and fast economic decline, have been steadily climbing up the list of countries from which cross-border adoptions most often take place.

Borders open, borders close. Wars ravage. Sensationalized news stories focus the world's attention on a particular country's orphans for a time, and then the sad spotlight moves elsewhere. International relations turn chilly, then warm. The flux of cross-border adoptions constantly changes.

But more important and less provocative than the geopolitical or economic backdrop is the unique cultural heritage that each cross-culturally adopted child will call her own. These kids are American (or Canadian or British, etc.), but they are also Chinese or Haitian, Indian or Colombian, Korean or Russian, Vietnamese or Kazakh, Guatemalan or Ukrainian. The extent to which she or her family chooses to explore and embrace her cultural and adoption history will vary according to individual interests and circumstances. At some level, however, the culture, traditions, and celebrations, the people and the beauty of her homeland will remain with her forever and shape who she is and who she will become.

To help you learn a little about who she is, we have listed, in order, the top ten countries from which Americans adopted abroad in 2003 (the list, which changes from year to year, is from the U.S. State Department's website) and described—very briefly—where she is from.

The People's Republic of China

Geography and Population

Into the third largest country in the world (only Russia and Canada have more land mass), China crowds the world's largest population, over one billion people. One out of every five people in the world lives in China. China (which the Chinese call *Zhongguo,* not the English name of China) also has the third largest river, the Yangtze, and four thousand miles of coastline along the Yellow, East China, and South China Seas. The country contains—and is partially contained by—a famous architectural, military, and geological feat called the Great Wall of China, built over a span of twenty-five years, two thousand years ago. The wall worms its way throughout the country for four thousand miles.

Bounded by Russia, North Korea, Mongolia, Tajikistan, Kyrgyzstan, Kazakhstan, Pakistan, Afghanistan, India, Nepal, Bhutan, Myanmar, Laos, and Vietnam, one may expect China to be an ethnic potpourri like the United States. Yet 93 percent of the Chinese people consider themselves to be Han Chinese, or direct descendants of China's Han dynasty. The remaining 7 percent of its citizens belong to one of fifty-five small ethnic minorities clustered mostly along China's borders. Despite the fact that the Chinese are ethnically unified, language remains a divisive factor. The official language is Mandarin, yet, even though written Chinese is the same throughout the entire country, only 70 percent of the population actually speaks Mandarin. The remaining citizens speak one or several of hundreds of languages and dialects that pepper the country. Many of these dialects are not understandable to each other and are not compatible with Mandarin.

After the Communist Party took power in 1949, it divided China into twenty-two provinces; five autonomous regions, including Tibet and Inner Mongolia; and two special administrative regions, Hong Kong and Macau. Beijing (once known as Peking) is the capital and seat of the government, and Shanghai is revered as China's largest, most cosmopolitan city.

History and Government

China is one of the world's oldest living civilizations. Its history is long and complex, replete with war, dynastic ruin, dramatic political takeovers, succession and accession, and ideological change. Each chronological component of its history merits volumes. This brief overview just highlights the critical turning points that led to the development of China today.

The Chinese culture dates back to 2000 B.C., although, reportedly, humans inhabited the region twenty thousand years ago. Between the years 1994 B.C. and 1912 A.D., fourteen dynasties ruled China. During the Ch'in dynasty, the Chinese people built the Great Wall. Buddhism was introduced and the government organized according to the tenets of Confucianism during the Han dynasty between 202 B.C. and 220 A.D. The T'ang dynasty, ruling from 618 until 907, brought about great artistic achievement. China's final dynasty, Manchu, fell from power in 1912, foundering in the face of foreign encroachment, national division, and opium.

Historically, China has maintained a policy of self-containment, holding itself relatively closed to foreign and outside influences. Yet in the early nineteenth century, the Manchu dynasty opened China's doors to foreign trade. Most of this trade took place with Great Britain and, at first, a majority of it entailed Great Britain importing Chinese products. But opium would soon equalize the balance of trade between the two countries.

The Manchu dynasty saw the destructive impact the drug was having on its people—some reports hold that in 1906, forty million Chinese people were addicted to opium—so it restricted trade of opium. This restriction led to the Opium War, lasting from 1839 to 1842. Great Britain attacked and won, and the resulting treaty opened many Chinese ports to foreign trade and ceded Hong Kong to Great Britain. A second Opium War followed, from 1856 to 1860, and China again found itself at the mercy of a British treaty opening even more Chinese ports to foreign trade and further loosening restrictions on opium imports.

The Manchu dynasty began to weaken amid the foreign infringement. The Taiping Rebellion (a revolt against dynastic rule) and the Chinese loss in the Sino-Japanese War over the control of Korea weakened the dynasty even further. Taking advantage of China's feeble government, the West initiated its Open Door Policy, officially stating that China was equally open to trade with all foreign countries. In practice, this policy resulted in spheres of influence of Western powers within China and led to the 1900 Boxer Rebellion, an attempt to suppress growing Western influence in China.

Although the rebellion against foreign power did not succeed, a 1911 rebellion against dynastic power did. The country overthrew the Manchu dynasty and installed Sun Yat-sen, a Western-educated physician, as a temporary president. A civil war ensued, pitting warlord-governed states against Sun Yat-sen's new party, the Kuomintang. The Kuomintang, or Nationalist Party, held power in the southern portion of China while the landholding warlords retained power in the north. In the meantime, in 1921 the Chinese Communist Party formed, and Sun Yat-sen cooperated with the party in order to secure aid from the Soviet Union.

When Chiang Kai-shek took over the Nationalist Party after Sun Yat-sen's death in 1925, he discontinued collusion with the Communist Party, expanded his party up north, and took over governing the entire country. The Nationalists and the Communists began warring over control of China. With help from Russia, after World War II, the Communist Party captured Manchuria and started pushing the Nationalists back. At the same time, the Communist Party began to rally grassroots support from a population fatigued by war and fed up with unstable rule. By 1949, the Communist Party conquered Beijing and set up a central Communist government. It forced Chiang Kai-shek and the Nationalist Party to Taiwan and officially formed the People's Republic of China on the mainland.

Mao Tse-tung, leading the new Communist government, immediately nationalized industry, collectivized agriculture, and tightened police power. He distributed food to a hungry population, brought inflation under control, recognized women as important party members, and organized the country into provinces and the people into work units. Rapid development followed.

But not all of the changes were positive. Mao subjected artists and intellectuals to strict scrutiny. His lip service to "Let One Hundred Flowers Bloom" and to permit intellectuals to criticize the government yielded so much "constructive criticism" that the government quickly changed its tune. Soon Mao and his followers were mandating thought reform and jailing or exiling individuals who dared to express negative views of the government.

The "Great Leap Forward" was Mao's attempt to revitalize China's agriculture in the 1950s. Workers gathered from all over the country, from both rural and urban settings, to embark on communal water control and irrigation projects. But rather than increasing output, bad weather and the withdrawal of Soviet support resulted in a devastating famine during which between thirty and sixty million people perished.

The 1966–1970 Cultural Revolution further weakened Mao's position within the party. It reportedly began after a theater released a play criticizing Mao's government. Consequently, Mao formed his own rudimentary army, called the Red Guards. This army rampaged the country, attacking, imprisoning, and killing intellectuals, educators, and artists. Mao halted publications and forbade religious practice. The Red Guards destroyed many significant Chinese feudal and dynastic works of art and architecture. Rather than strengthening his position within the government, the Cultural Revolution actually divided the government further between Maoists and those with more moderate ideals.

Mao died in 1976, and the Chinese government instituted some reforms directed toward economic growth and international cooperation. The strict Communism of the Mao days began to fade as some capitalist-like initiatives improved conditions. The 1989 Tiananmen Square incident—a peaceful protest that ended with government-sanctioned troops killing hundreds of student protesters—further chipped away at Communist ideals and support.

Economy

After Mao's death, the government began to focus on improving the economy, starting with the "Four Modernizations": industry, agriculture, defense, and science/technology, and in the last two decades of the twentieth century China made significant economic strides. For instance, when the government decollectivized agriculture (in which fifty percent of the population participates), production jumped. Foreign investment has increased as the economy has become more and more decentralized. China has gone more global, trading primarily with the United States, Japan, South Korea, and Germany, and it even entered the World Trade Organization in 2001. Growth has slowed in recent years, but the outlook remains positive.

Not surprisingly, and partially out of necessity, China is the world's largest producer of rice. It also holds that title with respect to wheat, cotton, tobacco, red meat, and coal. China is the world's fifth largest oil producer, but also has tremendous untapped offshore oil deposits that are currently being explored. Major industries, most of which are still state-owned and -run, include textiles, chemicals, plastics, electronics, and toys.

Culture and Holidays

Over centuries of political upheaval, the heart of Chinese culture—which is tied to, but not based on, religion—has remained strong and relatively static. Though China's government today permits religious freedom, it still discourages religious practice. Religion in China is a historic mix of Buddhism, Confucianism, and Taoism. But these bodies of thought have had profound effects on Chinese society beyond their spiritual and religious underpinnings. Specifically, the Confucian notions of respect for elders and authority, reverence for the past, and love for country have long been integral to mainstream Chinese culture. Family is the overriding priority. Even though some of the Communist changes—assigned workplaces far from families and required reporting of family members not loyal to the party—made filial piety more difficult "in practice," devotion to family has remained paramount.

Communism did not alter cultural mores like filial piety but it did change some specific Chinese traditions that take place within the family. For instance, families no longer bind women's feet and men do not freely take concubines into their homes. Also, before Communism, only 20 percent of the population was considered to be literate, most of them men. Now, with public education for males and females alike, 81.5 percent of the population is literate (93 percent if the sample excludes the elderly).

This increasing literacy rate is impressive considering the complexity of the Chinese language. Chinese has numerous dialects and a complex system of characters, rather than letters. The language contains many homonyms that, when written in English, look like the same word, but are distinguished in Chinese by the characters used to portray them and the tones used to pronounce them. There have been some proposed and some implemented controversial initiatives to simplify the characters in order to increase literacy. In order to translate Chinese words into other languages, translators use a pinyin, which romanizes the pronunciation of certain characters. Use of pinyin explains why in English there are several different spellings for many Chinese words. For instance, sometimes "Taoism" is spelled "Daoism" and sometimes "Mao Tse-tung" is spelled "Mao Zedong."

Other Chinese inventions less obtuse than their language have made their way west. For instance, the Chinese invented paper centuries before it traveled to Western civilizations. China also takes credit for inventing gunpowder, printing, and the mariner's compass. The West has imported aspects of traditional Chinese medicine, such as herbs and acupuncture. And in the reverse, China has integrated Western medicine into its own traditional methods to create its own unique brand of medical practice. *Feng shui*, currently popular in interior design, originated in China. Meaning "wind and water," feng shui is the process of directing an individual's *qi* (or energy) to create happiness and wealth.

Though a good portion of Chinese art was destroyed in the Cultural Revolution, art has been liberated since the days of Mao and is thriving in China today. Much of the modern art resembles traditional Chinese art and surprisingly little has changed in terms of discipline and technique. China boasts some of the world's finest ceramics. Calligraphy, China's traditional highest art form, is ubiquitous, decorating caves, temples, mountains, walls, and canvases. Chinese theater plays a tremendous role in culture, as illustrated in the famous Chinese film *Farewell My Concubine*. Theater in China is called opera because of the critical role music has played. Acrobatics and martial arts also factor prominently in Chinese opera. Moreover, China has a successful international film industry, based in Hong Kong; most of the films are of the kung fu variety. A number of these films out of Hong Kong have received international notice and acclaim.

Many of the Chinese holidays are based on the lunar calendar, which follows the cycles of the moon. The most celebrated holiday is the Lunar New Year, which takes place on the first day of the lunar calendar. The date on a Western calendar varies every year; it can be as early as January 21 or as late as February 19. Chinese people travel to get together with relatives and enjoy feasts, fireworks, parades, and costumes. They also exchange gifts, frequently contained in red envelopes. After fifteen days, the Lunar New Year celebration ends with the Festival of Lanterns, which features massive light shows and displays of paper lanterns of all different shapes and colors. The Dragon Boat Festival, which commemorates the anniversary of the death of Qu Yuan, a beloved minister to the Zhou emperor, is celebrated in the fifth moon. Around 221 B.C., Qu Yuan threw himself into the Milou River in his despair over the defeat of the emperor, and fishermen rushed into the river in long boats, beating drums to try to scare the fish away from his body. Today the holiday is celebrated around the world with boat races and festivities. Another holiday, the Moon Festival, is held in the fall on the fifteenth day of the eighth moon, and celebrates what is considered to be the most beautiful moon of the year. The festivities entail eating mooncakes and watching the moon with family.

Food

Chinese cuisine is quite famous worldwide, especially the Americanized, fast-food-like, half-sibling version of Chinese cuisine ubiquitous in this country. True Chinese cuisine is actually extremely diverse and is notable for both the quality and the quantity of its recipes. It has been said that the Chinese will prepare and eat "anything on four legs." That might be an exaggeration, but it's not that much of a stretch. Exotic animals, ranging from crickets to snakes to the now-banned civet cats, do feature in Chinese cuisine. And the Chinese tend to cook the entire animal. They won't serve a chicken breast; they'll serve the entire bird. Fish arrives whole—bones, eyes, and everything.

Exoticism is not the only characteristic of Chinese cooking, however. Appearance, color, and aroma are critical components in Chinese cuisine, each dish intentionally containing at least three to five different colors. Also, Chinese chefs sprinkle scallions, ginger, garlic, and chili pepper into many dishes as much for their distinct aromas as for their tastes.

China has eight different types of cuisine, divided by region. The Sichuan region, for instance, is known for its spicy and pungent dishes, such as Kung Pao chicken and smoked duck. Cantonese cuisine, another example, preserves flavor by employing braising and stir-frying techniques. In all of the regions, the people drink tea, and because they view knives and forks as cold and violent, they use chopsticks, which they perceive as gentler.

Interesting Fact

In 1974 archaeologists excavated an army of over six thousand terra cotta soldiers. These statues, built over two thousand years ago, stand guard over the massive tomb of Emperor Shi Huangdi of the Q'ing dynasty. Archaeologists continue to unearth more clay soldiers, horses, and chariots, and estimate that the entire tomb could extend for more than twenty square miles. The soldiers stand in Shaanxi province in Northwest China and have generated a well-worn tourist path into the region.

Literature and Other Books for Further Reading

An ancient Chinese proverb, "The palest ink is better than the best memory" reveals the importance the Chinese place on their tremendous body of written and literary work. Chinese proverbs, for instance, still used in daily life today, reveal a lot about Chinese culture and society. Two examples worth considering include: "A book holds a house of gold," and "When you have two pennies left in the world, buy a loaf of bread with one and a lily with the other." But China's written literature best reflects its history, struggles, and traditions. Unfortunately, most Chinese literature is untranslated and untranslatable into English, and the Communist regime—though less rigid than when under Mao—heavily controls the written content.

A Dream of Red Mansions (1978)

by Cao Xuequin; Yang Hsien-yi and Gladys Yang (Translators); Tai Tun-pang (Illustrator)

This epic Chinese classic novel, written in the middle of the eighteenth century, and translated only recently into several different English versions, recounts a tragic love affair in upscale urban China.

Red Azalea (1994), *Wild Ginger* (2002), *Becoming Madame Mao* (2000)

by Anchee Min

Each of these three mesmerizing modern novels/memoirs by Anchee Min, who was born in Shanghai and joined the Red Guard, depicts the lives of young people caught up in the Cultural Revolution.

Soul Mountain (2000)

by Gao Xingjian; Mabel Lee (Translator)

Based on this Nobel Prize winner's personal story, this novel by Gao Xingjian, who was also a celebrated Chinese playwright, critic, and painter before he left China to live in exile in Paris, is both a vivid account of travels through modern rural China and a metaphor for the soul of China itself.

Red China Blues: My Long March From Mao to Now (1996)

by Jan Wong

This is a work of journalism and a firsthand account of a Chinese-Canadian woman's perception of and experience with the Communist takeover in China.

The Good Earth (1931)

by Pearl S. Buck

This Pulitzer Prize–winning novel, written by an American missionary and humanitarian in China, famously depicts Chinese peasant life in the 1920s.

The Joy Luck Club (1989), *The Kitchen God's Wife* (1991), *The Hundred Secret Senses* (1995), *The Bonesetter's Daughter* (2001)
by Amy Tan

Amy Tan is probably this country's most well-known Chinese-American author of popular literature. Each of her bestselling works of fiction is based on her Chinese cultural ancestry.

The Lost Daughters of China: Abandoned Girls, Their Journey to America and the Search for a Missing Past (2000)
by Karin Evans; Preface by Anchee Min

A thoughtful and moving exploration of Chinese culture and the cross-border adoption of Chinese girls.

River Town: Two Years on the Yangtze
by Peter Hessler (2001)

Written by a young American Peace Corps volunteer in 1996, this book captures, with grace and humor, the marked cultural differences between the East and the West and expresses the author's fondness for the Chinese people.

Russia

Geography and Population

Neither entirely Eastern nor Western, Russia is the largest country in the world and straddles two continents, Asia and Europe. The land of Russia ranges from the treeless tundra in the north (covered by permafrost, permanently frozen soil), to belts of coniferous forests, grassy plains called steppes, and semidesert and mountain areas in the south. Bordering the Baltic Sea, the Black Sea, and the Pacific and Arctic Oceans, Russia is also home to 120,000 rivers and 200,000 lakes, including the largest lake in the world (the Caspian Sea, a saltwater lake that lies ninety-two feet below sea level) and the deepest lake in the world (Lake Baikal, which plunges down 5,315 feet). Known for its long and bitter winters that have turned approaching invaders away, including Napoleon's army in 1812 and Adolf Hitler in World War II, Russia also has hot, subtropical regions around the Black Sea. A train trip between Moscow in the west and Vladivostok in the east takes seven days and passes through eight time zones.

The people of Russia are distributed unevenly throughout the country, about three-fourths living in urban areas west of the Ural Mountains. Two of Russia's cities—Moscow and St. Petersburg—each have more than four million inhabitants. More than 80 percent of Russia's 150 million people are of Russian ancestry. The remaining 20 percent comprise over 100 other nationality groups, including: Tatars (or Tartars), Ukrainians, Chuvash, Bashkirs, Belarusians, Mordvins, Chechen, Germans, Udmurts, Mari, Kazakhs, Avars, Armenians, and Jews (who are considered a nationality). Remote northern parts of the country are also inhabited by small Siberian groups, including Inuit, also called Eskimos. Russian is the official language and is written in the Cyrillic alphabet.

History and Government

The history of Russia is as vast as its land and as turbulent as its weather. For hundreds of years Russia was ruled by czars and empresses, who had complete control over most aspects of Russian life. During this rule, most Russians were poor, uneducated peasants relegated to serfdom. Czarist Russian history reads like an incestuous Romanov soap opera—from Peter the Great having his son Alexis sentenced to death for treason to Catherine the Great's decadent parties and many rumored lovers—with infighting, uprisings, takeovers, and great economic striation.

In 1917, during World War I, revolutionaries overthrew the czarist government and formed a provisional Communist government headed by Vladimir Lenin. In 1922, after three years of civil war between the Communists and anti-Communists, the Russian government and three other republics formed a new nation called the Union of Soviet Socialist Republics (USSR), also known as the

Soviet Union.

After Lenin's death in 1924, Joseph Stalin came to power. Stalin collectivized farms, bureaucratized industry, and suppressed religion, art, and literature. He also instituted the Great Purge, in which secret police arrested millions of people, killing them or sending them off to prison camps. Nevertheless, the Soviet Union emerged from World War II a stronger political force, becoming the "other superpower" in the world. As the Soviet Union entered the Cold War—a decades-long rivalry between East and West characterized by mutual distrust and suspicion—it began to invest in its military to the neglect of all other areas. Stalin left this neglectful legacy when he died in 1953, and it was not until Mikhail Gorbachev became head of the Communist Party in 1985 and was elected to the newly created office of president of the Soviet Union in 1990 that the reality of living in the Soviet Union was revealed: the poverty, the unemployment, the corruption.

Opposition to the Soviet government grew. The Berlin Wall—the symbol of Soviet domination—fell in 1989, and with the force of its fall, any pretense of continued Soviet domination in both Eastern Europe and constituent republics of the USSR evaporated. Demanding more self-government, most of the Soviet republics declared their independence in the 1990s. At the end of 1991, Boris Yeltsin, the newly elected Russian president, and the presidents of Belarus and Ukraine declared that the Soviet Union had ceased to exist and announced the formation of the Commonwealth of Independent States (CIS), a group of independent countries tied by economic and defense links. On December 25, 1991, Gorbachev resigned as Soviet president, and the Soviet Union ended. The current Russian government follows a voter-approved 1993 constitution and has three branches: an elected president, a parliament led by a prime minister, and a judiciary branch modeled on the French system.

Economy

Since the fall of the Soviet Union in 1991, Russia has worked to shift its state-controlled economy to a market-controlled economy. As it struggled—and continues to struggle—through the turmoil of transforming itself into a democratic, capitalist nation, Russia fell into an economic crisis in 1998. Its economy recovered, based in part on increasing exports of oil and metals, but modern reforms still have not eased the hardships of many of the Russian people. About 25 percent of the population continues to live in poverty.

Although the country is rich with natural resources, many of its resources are in remote, difficult-to-navigate areas. Russia produces 17 percent of the world's oil, 30 percent of the world's natural gas, and much of its coal, iron, and timber. Russia's large ocean fishing fleet accounts for one-quarter of the world's fresh fish and one-third of the world's canned fish. Many consider caviar produced from the sturgeon of the Caspian Sea to be the best in the world. Even with only 8 percent of its land arable, agriculture is productive, yielding stores of wheat, barley, oats, potatoes, and sunflowers. And although its industrial infrastructure is antiquated and the manufacturing capacity is set up to build what have become unnecessary arms, Russia is prepared for the information age. Over 40 percent of its population are college educated, placing Russia among the most educated countries in the world.

Culture and Holidays

Art seems to flow in Russian blood. From performance to painting to literature, Russians have pioneered artistic endeavors for centuries. Art, in its various forms in Russia, sits at the very heart of Russian culture and tradition.

Although Italy receives more attention in this realm, it is Russia that has long been the center of iconic painting. For centuries, Russian Orthodox painters would fast before starting to paint and pray while painting each particular work. The images are intended not to reflect reality, but rather to aid in meditation and prayer. The twentieth century saw a resurgence of this type of art in Russia. Also religious in nature are the most famous buildings of Russian architecture: Russia's many-domed churches—some bearing the distinctive onion dome—dot the entire country. These churches, along with other religious themes, are the subjects of many of the miniature scenes gingerly painted on the uniquely Russian lacquered boxes.

Aside from its fine art and architecture, Russia has also earned fame for its folk art. For example, *dymkovo* toys are colorful, patterned clay display figures, and *matrioshka* are the seemingly infinite doll sets featuring smaller and smaller dolls that fit snugly inside their larger, otherwise identical counterparts.

Russian performance art takes center stage in its culture as well. Ballet and theater (even circus acts and figure skating) are at the heart of Russia's artistic soul. Russia has given the world some of the most well-known works of ballet: Tchaikovsky's *Swan Lake*, *The Nutcracker Suite,* and *The Sleeping Beauty* and Stravinsky's *The Firebird.* Modern ballet legends Rudolph Nureyev, Anna Pavlova, and Mikhail Baryshnikov all hail from Russia. The leading ballet companies, which continue to perform today, are the Kirov Ballet (formerly the Russian Imperial Ballet) of St. Petersburg and the Bolshoi Ballet of Moscow.

One of the world's most famous playwrights, Anton Chekhov—whose plays *The Cherry Orchard*, *Uncle Vanya,* and *The Seagull* are still produced every year in theaters large and small across the United States—wrote his plays in nineteenth-century Russia. Another Russian theater master, Stanislavsky, an actor and director, was so influential throughout the world that his acting technique—known as "the Method"—inspired several longstanding American schools of acting and informs some of Hollywood's greats, including Marlon Brando, Robert DeNiro, Al Pacino, and Dustin Hoffman.

The fall of Communism spurred an interest in all types of pre-Soviet art and performance. At the same time, it also released the taboo from religion. The Russian Orthodox Church, sixty million strong, is the largest religious denomination in the country, and January 7, the Russian Orthodox Christmas, is a national holiday. In a Christmas ceremony called Kolyadki, families make a "snow lady," using a carrot for the nose, prunes for the eyes, and green beans for the teeth. They then dance around the snow lady with torches, singing traditional songs.

Russians also celebrate several folk festivals and the typical national holidays, such as Independence Day on June 12. One folk holiday, Troitsa, which takes place seven weeks after Easter, entails decorating houses with greenery and placing flowers in water for fortune telling. The festivities also include dressing birch trees with the clothing of unmarried women, followed by singing and dancing around the clothed trees.

Food

The traditional Russian diet is hearty, although eating habits are changing with the advent of convenience and fast food. A typical Russian meal starts with an appetizer of fish jelly or salted herring, served with horseradish and other condiments. For a special occasion the appetizer might include caviar. Soup is generally the first course. *Schi* (soup with cabbage); borscht; and *rassolniki* (soup with pickled cucumbers) are popular. Meat and fish dishes—such as beef stroganoff, mutton stew, suckling pig, baked sturgeon, and fried pike—are served with vegetables and potatoes or *kasha* (cooked buckwheat). Bread, including *blinis* (thin pancakes served with filling), accompanies every meal. Russians drink large quantities of tea, but coffee is becoming more popular.

The Russian saying, "There can only be not enough vodka," characterizes the importance of vodka to Russian cuisine and culture. Russia began to distill vodka in the 1400s; it had the resources—birch trees and barley—needed to make it in large quantities. In fact, the vodka trade supports entire regions of the country.

Interesting Fact

It is tradition in Russia that when a couple gets married, someone presents them with a loaf of bread at their wedding. Both members of the couple take a bite of the bread and the member of the couple who takes the larger bite becomes the head of the household.

Literature and Other Books for Further Reading

Russian literature includes some of the greatest masterpieces ever written. From Tolstoy's *War and Peace* and *Anna Karenina* to Dostoevsky's *Crime and Punishment* and *The Brothers Karamazov*, Russian novels and poems have engaged the world with their universal themes about social mores, war, God, moral duty, and love set against vivid backdrops of Russian history. The greatest Russian works were written during the artistic and cultural revival of the mid to late 1800s, before Communist government censors imposed strict limits on what was published.

The Captain's Daughter and Other Stories (1961)
by Alexander Pushkin; Introduction by Natalie Duddington (Translator)

Considered by some to be Russia's greatest writer, Pushkin was one of the first to depict stories of Russian realism. This esteemed collection of stories is from the early to mid-nineteenth century.

Doctor Zhivago (1958)
by Boris Pasternak; Max Hayward and Manya Harari (Translators)

Pasternak's epic love story, set amidst the turmoil of the Russian Revolution, was translated into many languages and published abroad to international acclaim, even though the Russian government forbade the novel's publication and forced Pasternak to renounce the 1958 Nobel Prize for Literature.

Favorite Russian Fairy Tales (1995)
by Arthur Ransome; Simon Galkin (Illustrator)

These stories and fairy tales have been a part of Russian culture for centuries. Six tales of witches and wizardry, perilous journeys, wise animals, frightful giants, and beautiful princesses—among them, the legendary Fire-Bird, the dulcimer-playing Sadko, the iron-toothed witch Baba Yaga, and a goat that sneezes gold pieces.

Peter and the Wolf (1936)
by Sergei Prokofiev

This classic Russian children's symphonic fairy tale has been reissued by everyone from Sesame Street's Big Bird to U2's Bono.

Natasha's Dance: A Cultural History of Russia (2002)
by Orlando Figes

Beginning in the eighteenth century with the building of St. Petersburg and culminating with the Soviet regime, Figes introduces Russian history by examining how writers, artists, and musicians grappled with Russia's image. The book weaves the great works by Dostoevsky, Stravinsky, and Chagall with folk embroidery, peasant songs, religious icons, and all the customs of daily life, to reveal the spirit of "Russianness."

The Cambridge Companion to Modern Russian Culture (1998)
Nicholas Rzhevsky (Editor)

This compendium of essays introduces Russian culture in all its rich diversity in the context of its history and political changes.

The Republic of Guatemala

Geography and Population

Guatemala houses more people than any other Central American country. Only a tiny fraction of this country's approximately thirteen million citizens, however, claims over half of the country's wealth. But what the people of Guatemala do not possess in material fortune, they do enjoy in cultural riches.

A country about the size of Kentucky, Guatemala does not have the most generous proportions to contain its large population. While most of its citizens reside in the small upper highlands region, about two million live in and around the capital, Guatemala City.

The people of Guatemala are divided into two main groups: Indians and people of mixed Spanish and Indian ancestry. About half of Guatemalans are Indians, descended from the ancient Mayan civilizations, and most are poor and uneducated. The other half, Guatemalans of mixed Spanish and Indian ancestry, are called *ladinos,* and although many of them are poor as well, ladinos almost exclusively constitute the middle and upper classes of Guatemalan society and occupy the powerful positions in government and business. Spanish is the official language of Guatemala, but the Mayan groups bring over twenty different indigenous, primary languages to the mix.

Guatemala is crunched between Honduras, El Salvador, Mexico, and Belize, with whom it has shared strained relations and tense land disputes over the years. The Caribbean Sea and the North Pacific Ocean also border the country. Just like the state of Maryland is the self-proclaimed "America in Miniature" because of its smaller-scale but nationally representative topography, Guatemala could be "Central America in Miniature." It contains the region's highest peak—an inactive volcano called Tajumulco—along with vast Mayan ruins, Caribbean coastline, tropical rainforests, dramatic Pacific surf, lowland forest, swamps, and river valleys.

History and Government

Guatemala's distant past shone so brightly that it carried the Guatemalans through the country's recent past of corruption, instability, unrest, and disappointment. The Mayan civilization, of which Guatemala was the heart, flourished from the fifth through the eighth centuries, culturally and intellectually. Building pyramids, temples, and acropolises throughout the country, the Mayans excelled in architecture. Also, their emphasis on math and science led these ancients to develop a calendar more accurate than the one the Europeans were using during medieval times.

By the early sixteenth century, however, the strength of the Mayan civilization had dissipated, leaving the country vulnerable. The Spanish took advantage of this vulnerability when they arrived in 1523. Spanish conquistadors colonized Guatemala and used their military superiority to kill and enslave many natives. Thus began the enduring repression of the indigenous people of Guatemala.

Centuries later, in 1821, Guatemala gained independence from Spain. The country briefly became a territory of Mexico and then, also briefly, a part of the United Provinces of Central America. Guatemala's total independence—and its search to find its political identity—launched a century of political change, instability, and strife.

By the mid-twentieth century, after far too many years of one government wrestling control from another, the Guatemalan people were ready for a change. This drive led to the Ten Years of Spring, from 1944 to 1954. During this ephemeral period, Guatemala enjoyed a representative government with two consecutive elected presidents. These presidents attempted to initiate change, free expression, unionization for workers, and other social and economic reforms.

But, alas, the unstable international climate interfered with Guatemala's flirtation with political stability. Fearing a strengthening Communist influence in the Guatemalan government, an insurgent group, backed by the United States, overthrew this elected government and halted the popular reforms. From this overthrow emerged a corrupt, right-wing militarized government that consumed Guatemalan public services, such as the police force. Over the next thirty-six years, this government incited and then repressed organized groups of left-wing guerrilla insurgents through assassinations and forced exiles. The Mayan civilians were caught in the political and literal crossfire, and many died. This civil war reportedly led to the deaths of over 200,000 Guatemalans.

In the late 1980s, this massacre caught international attention, and by 1996 the Guatemalan government signed a peace agreement ending the civil unrest. The new government put into place at the time of the peace accord is based upon a constitution written in 1985 and revised in 1993. This constitution calls for a representative government with three separate branches, a president, a civil law system, a legislative house, judicial review, and the right to vote.

Economy

Guatemala has only recently been able to offer peace and a stable government as attractions for potential foreign investors, but the 1996 peace accord did lead to an influx of foreign investment. The United States is the country's biggest trading partner; El Salvador, Mexico, Japan, and Germany also invest in and trade with Guatemala. Exports include sugar, coffee, and bananas. (In 1906 the United Fruit Company, now Chiquita Brands International, an American firm, began developing plantations in Guatemala.) Increasingly gaining steam are textiles, apparel, winter vegetables, flowers, and natural rubber. Guatemala also has its share of natural resources, boasting nickel and petroleum deposits, as well as zinc and lead concentrates. Tourism is a growing industry, and as peace becomes more entrenched in Guatemala, its growth promises to accelerate.

The economy has been slowly picking up in recent years, and improvements to the country's infrastructure could spur additional economic development. For instance, even though only one-quarter of the gross domestic earnings comes from agriculture, over half of the population still toils in agricultural pursuits. Illiteracy plagues 40 percent of the population, as does lack of educational opportunity, inferior roads, and lackluster communications systems. These problems exacerbate, and are exacerbated by, the fact that over 75 percent of the Guatemalan population lives in poverty.

Culture and Holidays

The majority of Guatemalans practice Roman Catholicism, with a sizable minority (around 35 percent) observing Pentecostal Protestant faiths. Many of the Mayan cultures mix aspects of traditional indigenous religions with Catholicism. The result is a country that is almost always observing a festival of some kind. Semana Santa (Holy Week), which falls in April, is one of the most honored occasions, and the city of Antigua holds the most internationally renowned celebration, performing a detailed reenactment of the crucifixion of Christ that includes a mock trial and funeral procession. Rabin Ajau (July 27) is the country's largest traditional Mayan festival. For a week in July, they celebrate with traditional food and dance and a beauty pageant showcasing traditional Mayan dress. The Guatemalans celebrate All Saints Day on November 1 by walking to a cemetery and flying giant kites with notes attached to them. The notes are written to loved ones who have passed away.

Despite centuries of repression and, more recently, decades of violence, the indigenous people of Guatemala have held tenaciously to their roots, culture, and traditions. They speak their own languages, practice their own hybrid religions, listen to traditional marimba music, and dress in traditional garb. On the other hand, the ladinos often identify more with their Spanish roots, speaking Spanish, practicing Catholicism, and dressing like Europeans. This duality, characterized by Spanish technical skills and Mayan color, often interweaves to produce an interesting and unique way of perceiving the world.

Food

The duality of cultures also affects the foods Guatemalans eat. For urban dwellers—mostly ladinos—a mix of European and indigenous foods prevails so that in a given meal, they may eat American-style fast food combined with time-honored rice and beans. The rural indigenous population eats traditional fare, which includes corn, beans, chicken, fruits, and vegetables, and on festive occasions, beef and pork.

Some of the more customary dishes combine Caribbean and Mexican influences. *Chiles rellenos,* or chiles stuffed with meat, are popular for celebrations. Guatemalans also eat *taquitos,* which are stuffed, rolled, and fried tortillas; *caldo de pata,* cow's foot soup; and *pollo en pipian,* chicken in a pumpkin seed sauce. *Ceviche,* a popular indigenous dish of marinated raw fish, has crossed borders and dots the menus of many American and European restaurants. Dessert comes in many varieties, but ingredients often include plantains or baked bananas.

Interesting Fact

One can tell a lot about a Mayan woman by the clothes she wears. For centuries, indigenous Guatemalan women have been weaving their clothing on portable backstrap looms, which get their name from the belt or strap support that fits around the back of the weaver, who controls the tension of the warp with her body. Not only are these traditional weavings boldly colorful and intricate, but they bear meaningful messages encoded into their designs. Each design and color is unique to a specific village or individual, and the designs give clues as to the wearer's home village, cultural identity, religious beliefs, and even familial ties.

Literature and Other Books for Further Reading

Guatemala has produced a number of well-respected authors, including two who have won Nobel Prizes for literature. Here is a sampling of their work, as well as some additional reading on the country itself.

I, Rigoberta Menchu: An Indian Woman in Guatemala (1984)
by Rigoberta Menchu; Introduction by Elisabeth Burgos-Debray (Editor); Ann Wright (Translator)

This book, told orally by Nobel Prize winner Rigoberta Menchu to an anthropologist who translated it, tells the story of traditional village life in Guatemala, amidst the backdrop of civil war and poverty. Menchu celebrates her culture and traditions in the face of the repression and brutality wrought by warring governments and discrimination.

Men of Maize (1975)
by Miguel Angel Asturias; Gerald Martin (Translator)

This Nobel Prize–winning book tells of the cultural and political clashes in Guatemala in the twentieth century by focusing on Indian village life. The author draws a realistic picture of Guatemala and its Indian cultures.

Abuela's Weave (1993)
by Omar Castenada; Enrique O. Sanchez (Illustrator)

This children's book set in Guatemala features a grandmother teaching her granddaughter about the Mayan traditions and tapestry weaving. It also teaches lessons about family pride and personal growth.

Silence on the Mountain: Stories of Terror, Betrayal, and Forgetting in Guatemala (2002)
by Daniel Wilkinson

This work of investigative journalism explores Guatemalan society during its decades of civil war. The author gives voice to many Guatemalans who lived through, but were unable to talk about, what happened during the internal struggle.

The Republic of Korea (a.k.a. South Korea)

Geography and Population

South Korea, a peninsula that is about the size of Indiana, packs in a population of 25.5 million people, one of the most dense in the world. Aside from its size, a unique characteristic of this country's population is its lack of uniqueness. All Koreans are believed to have descended from a single Mongolian bloodline, and there are no significant minorities in the country. Such homogeneity is a rare trait for a country to possess in times of easy mobility and global exchange. Although aging and declining, this population of universally shared language, religion, culture, geography, and historical "hard times" has bred interpersonal solidarity and a oneness between people and country.

Nevertheless, the South Korean peninsula itself seems to belie the uniformity of its residents and founders. Covered almost entirely by mountains and dissected by numerous navigable waterways, South

Korea's topography appears to be quite diverse. The country is separated from China by the Yellow Sea and from Japan by the Sea of Japan, more wisely referred to around Koreans as the East Sea. Off its coast, South Korea comprises 3,420 mostly uninhabited islands. South Korea's capital, Seoul, houses a large chunk of the Korean people who flocked to the cities during the industrialization of the 1960s and 1970s. Many of these same people are now fleeing to the suburbs.

History and Government

South Korea refers to itself as the Land of the Morning Calm, but from a look at the country's history, this appellation sounds more like wishful thinking than an accurate description. Dating its origins back as far as 2333 B.C., Korea first formed a unified country in the seventh century under the Silla Kingdom. Korea had been an independent nation for many centuries by the time that Japan invaded and took over in the sixteenth century. Throughout that and the next century, Japan and China took turns invading and ruling Korea. In fact, relations between Korea and Japan today are still tense because of the brutal manner in which Japan ruled Korea.

After ridding itself of the presence of its powerful neighbors in the seventeenth century, Korea isolated itself from the outside world, becoming so insular that it earned the nickname the "Hermit Kingdom." Korea successfully closed itself off until 1906, when once again Japan stepped in, this time annexing the peninsula. Harsh Japanese rule lasted until the end of World War II, when Japan was required to leave Korea.

But the country's troubles were only just beginning. In the spoils of World War II, a United Nations–supported government took over the southern portion of the peninsula, while a Chinese- and USSR-backed government took over the northern half. When the south declared its independence, the north invaded. The ensuing Korean War, which literally pitted geographically disparate family members against each other, lasted until 1953. That year brought on a cease-fire and coined the term for the heavily armed territory between North and South Korea, the "demilitarized zone." Two million people died in the war, and the country was officially divided.

South Korea then plunged into several decades of civilian protest and political instability, swinging from democracy to military rule and back again. Finally, in the late 1980s, President Chun granted the wishes of the protesters for democratic elections, and the country started in the direction of the democracy it is today. Since 1998, South Korea has had a democratic president, a legislative body, and a constitutional republic.

Economy

Initially after partition, South Korea stumbled financially. It had been the center of agriculture, not industry, and, with the exception of tungsten and graphite, fish, and rice paddies, North Korea contained most of the peninsula's resources. But the country quickly regained its footing and has since enjoyed five decades of impressive economic growth.

South Korea began to stir economically by producing consumer goods such as apparel. It continued developing its industrial base by delving into heavier industry like electronic equipment, cars, chemicals, and ships. Hyundais, for instance, have become popular throughout the world. The United States, Japan, and the European Union became major trading partners with Korea. With the exception of the financial crisis in Asia in 1997, during which South Korea sought aid from the International Monetary Fund, the South Korean economy has climbed, exports have increased, and the array of products manufactured in the country has broadened. What was once primarily an agricultural region now records only 9 percent of its workforce in the agricultural sector; 71 percent of South Korean employees are now working in service industries.

Culture and Holidays

South Koreans base their year on the lunar calendar, and many of their holidays correspond to that calendar. A majority of Koreans practice either Buddhism or Christianity, adding to the long list of recognized holidays. Seollal, the lunar new year, which takes place on the first day of the first moon, is one of South Korea's most festive celebrations. Families assemble to hold ancestral ceremonies, pledge obedience to elders, and enjoy a feast. Another holiday stemming from the lunar calendar is Chuseok, or Harvest Moon Festival. This holiday, held on the fifteenth day of the eighth lunar month, is the Korean equivalent of the American Thanksgiving, and also entails honoring ancestors.

The South Koreans celebrate Buddha's birthday, which usually falls in May, by parading through villages with lanterns. The country observes national holidays like Independence Day and Labor Day. They even have a holiday called Hangeul Day, which occurs on October 9th and honors the start of the Korean alphabet.

Many South Koreans live their lives based on an ethical system propounded by the Chinese philosopher Confucius. They place a high value on serenity and being at one with their country and with nature. South Koreans devote themselves to what they call the "Five Relationships." They focus their respect exclusively on these relationships, which helps to explain why outsiders (those not falling into any of these relationships) may find the South Koreans to be distant or dismissive. The relationships include ruler and subject; father and son; husband and wife; old and young; and friends. Within these relationships, the South Koreans highly value fidelity, filial piety, family, and social order. With respect to social order, younger generations—as demarked by ten-year age differences—must demonstrate respect to older generations by bowing and using the honorific references that are embedded in the Korean language.

Art is also an important aspect of South Korean culture. Despite their pride in their ethnic homogeneity, the Koreans have incorporated influences from many other cultures and traditions into their art forms. Traditional music, called *Chongak* and *Minsogak*, has Chinese influence and uses a mixture of string instruments. Traditional painting also has Chinese influence in that it uses brush-lines and calligraphy. The Koreans consider their language to be an art form, so characters often find their way into paintings.

The South Koreans perform and voraciously watch different types of dance, including mask, monk, and spirit cleansing. Modern dance performances are increasingly popular. Tae kwon do, originally a Korean self-defense martial art, has now become an international spectator sport. And, interestingly, the South Koreans also hold serious tug-of-war competitions.

Food

Korean food is considered to be atypical for Asia because it tends to be spicy and salty. Rice is the main staple, and fish, because of its plentiful supply around the peninsula, is the main source of protein. A typical Korean meal generally includes *kimchi*, which is cabbage pickled in brine and spices. The Koreans often serve *bulgogi*—Korean barbecue—on special occasions. The South Koreans drink rice wine, traditional teas like date tea, and *soju*, which is alcohol distilled from sweet potatoes. For dessert, they may enjoy *hotteok*, flat, fried cakes filled with cinnamon and sugar syrup. For the most part, South Koreans eat with chopsticks and a spoon.

Interesting Fact

Many South Koreans believe in divination—or fortune telling—and they plan major events in their lives around the outcomes of such readings. Fortune-tellers look to a number of sources to predict the future, including natural elements like rain and stars, animals or plants, dreams, physical attributes, and the results of certain sports events. South Koreans often consult fortune-tellers before exams, business matters, and even before deciding on a marriage partner.

Geomancy is a type of divination that gives the expression "location, location, location" new meaning: it is the method by which South Koreans determine where to build homes, locate offices or cemeteries, and expand cities. Geomancy tests the earth's energy and vibrations and considers topography in order to find ideal sites to build. For example, Seoul, which is surrounded by mountains, is considered to be in an ideal spot. South Koreans will often attribute misfortune to poorly selected sites.

Literature and Other Books for Further Reading

Korea has a rich tradition in literature, folk stories, and mythology. Many of the works have never been translated into English. The following lists some of the better known Korean works of literature, as well as some sources to consult for more information on the country and its people.

Evening Glow (2003)
by Won-il Kim; Agnita M. Tennant (Translator)

> This novel, from the perspective of a man growing up in post–World War II Korea, explores the political, cultural, and familial implications of the instability of the time before and after partition.

The Preview and Other Stories (2003)
by Son-Jak Cho; Chan Young Kim and David C. Carter (Translators)

Through the eyes of a young boy, this novella tells the story of modern Korea, after the Korean War. It captures the values of the people and their loyalty to one another and to their country.

The Koreans: Who They Are, What They Want, Where Their Future Lies (2004)
by Michael Breen

This book provides a modern look at Korean culture, economy, and society from the viewpoint of a veteran British journalist.

Red Bean Granny and the Tiger (1997)
by Dae-In Joh; Lee Choon-ok and John H. T. Harvey (Translators)

Through use of humor and childlike characters, this popular children's book teaches the lesson that the weak, by joining together, can overcome the powerful.

I Wish For You a Beautiful Life: Letters From the Korean Birth Mothers of Ae Ran Won to Their Children (1999)
Sara Dorow (Editor)

Heartbreaking messages of love, loss, and hope written by Korean birth mothers who have given up their children for adoption.

The Republic of Kazakhstan

Geography and Population

The Republic of Kazakhstan does not get a lot of media attention in the United States and the West, so it may surprise people to discover that it is the world's ninth largest country, that it spans two continents—Asia and Europe—and that it boasts 48,000 lakes and 2,000 miles of uninterrupted coastline along the Caspian Sea. Its unique location in West Central Asia positions it around the Ural Sea, west of which is Europe. So, a small part of Kazakhstan does in fact reside in Europe.

The country's makeup and culture, however, more closely identify with its Asian mass. Kazakhstan's bordering neighbors include China and Russia, as well as the lesser known Turkmenistan, Uzbekistan, and Kyrgystan. The official language of the country is Kazakh, but many citizens speak Russian either as a first or second language because up until 1991, Kazakhstan was under Soviet rule and Russian was its official language. Ethnic Kazakhs make up about 51 percent of the country's fifteen million people, with Russians representing about 30 percent. The remainder of the population resembles that of the United States in its melting-pot diversity. Some of the larger minorities include Ukrainians, Germans, Chechens, Kurds, and Koreans.

Its land varies as much as the ethnic backgrounds of its population. Kazakhstan borders the Caspian Sea to the west, is protected by mountains to the south and east, contains lowlands in the north and west, and has hills and steppes in its center. The majority of the country is flatland and desert.

History and Government

The ethnic Kazakhs were a nomadic people, living in tribes and migrating with the seasons to locate pastures for their herds. They resided in *yurts,* which are portable tents made of boiled camel's wool. In the eighteenth century, Russia conquered Kazakhstan and held the country under its rule until 1925, when it became the Kazakh Autonomous Soviet Socialist Republic and a member of the Union of Soviet Socialist Republics (USSR). The USSR encouraged Russians to settle the region, which explains the large Russian population there today. Kazakhstan existed under Communist rule as part of the USSR, until 1991, when it became an independent nation. In that year, the country joined the Commonwealth of Independent States, along with ten other former Soviet republics; it replaced the Communist government with a democracy; it drafted a new constitution; it formed a parliament; and it named a president.

Economy

Kazakhstan's economy has been flourishing over the last decade, since it declared its independence. Its success can be attributed in part to the country's enthusiasm over—and encouragement of—Western investment. But the bulk of Kazakhstan's success is attributed to its highly untapped and plentiful resources. Not only does the country offer a variety of quality agricultural products (dairy, leather, meat, wool, barley, cotton, rice, and wheat) and manufacture chemicals, textiles, and heavy machinery, but it also stores generous reserves of oil, gas, and commercial minerals inside its borders. In 2000, miners discovered oil in the Kazakh territory of the Caspian Sea. It turned out to be the largest oil find in thirty years and was a boon to the Kazakh economy.

Culture and Holidays

The commercial center of economic activity, and the country's largest city, Almaty, also houses a large concentration of the population of Kazakhstan. The diverse ethnicities there contribute to a varied religious and cultural makeup. The ethnic Kazakhs are Muslims and the ethnic Russians are Christian Orthodox, and each celebrate their own separate religious holidays and cultures. For example, the Muslims celebrate Oraza, which spans a month each winter. During that month, observers can only eat in the very early morning or the very late evening. The month ends with Ait—three days of eating, drinking, and celebrating. Likewise, the Russians have significantly influenced the Kazakhstan cities through their ballet, theater, and art.

The entire population celebrates the country's national holidays, many of which honor the country's relatively recent independence. The Kazakhs recognize a Day of the City, Kazakh Independence Day, Day of Unity of the People of Kazakh, Victory Day, Constitution Day, and Republic Day. Their New Year's Day, on the first of January, resembles the Western Christmas celebration because it features a brightly decorated "New Year's Tree" as well as presents and family get-togethers.

The Kazakhs celebrate the first day of the Eastern calendar, March 22, as the beginning of spring. The people honor this holiday with parades, festivals, national dishes, concerts, and games. The country also observes a holiday known as Women's Day on the eighth of March, which acknowledges the contribution women make and have made to the Kazakh culture and society.

Kazakhs commemorate these occasions in their own unique manner. Gatherings often feature folk songs and singing competitions. Singing has traditionally featured prominently in their traditions, as has storytelling. The Kazakh people tell legends and recite epics to entertain themselves and to mark special events. Interestingly, the horse as a symbol connotes meaning to the Kazakh people and figures in some capacity into all of their celebrations, either in the food, or in their activities, such as horseback games and races.

Food

The Kazakh people pride themselves on entertaining and view offering food to guests as the highest form of hospitality—the more food, the better the hospitality. Because Kazakhstan has had an influx of people of different ethnicities, its food has reaped the benefits of this variety, borrowing from Uzbek, Russian, Tatar, and Korean influences. Nevertheless, Kazakhstan has retained its own traditional style of cuisine.

The country's specialty is boiled horsemeat. Kazakhs perceive the horse as an important symbol and therefore strive to include it in many aspects of their lives, including culinary consumption. Typical dishes include horsemeat sausage and sheep intestines. The national dish is *besparmak*, which features chunks of horsemeat, served on the bone, atop noodles. The word means "five fingers" in Kazakh and symbolizes the manner in which the people eat the dish—with their fingers.

Interesting Fact

On special occasions at a Kazakh family table, one may encounter the ceremonial serving of a sheep's head. Generally, they do not serve the head to eat as a part of the meal. Rather, they cut off specific parts and offer them to members of the party. For example, they often cut off one of the sheep's ears and give it to the youngest person at the table. This offering symbolizes the host's wish that the young person will learn to listen well to his or her elders.

Literature and Other Books for Further Reading

Kazakh written literature is of fairly recent vintage because, typical of a nomadic culture, oral storytelling was a much more richly embedded tradition. Presently, Kazakh literature is thriving, but it mostly has not been translated into English. The following list includes several works of fiction that illuminate aspects of Kazakh life and history, along with a few works of nonfiction that serve as good primers on the Kazakh culture, history, politics, and people.

The Day Lasts More Than a Hundred Years (1983)
by Chingiz Aitmatov; Foreword by Katerina Clark; John French (Translator)

This novel, set in Kazakhstan, offers insight into Kazakh politics, culture, and humanity.

Kazakh Folksongs: From the Two Ends of the Steppe (2001)
by Janos Sipos; Dávid Somfai Kara and Éva Csáki (Contributors); Judit Pokaly (Translator)

This compilation offers a look into Kazakh culture through folk songs, one of its traditional and still popular means of communicating and celebrating.

The Soul of Kazakhstan (2001)

Photographs by Wayne Eastep; text by Alma Kunanbay; Gareth L. Steen (Editor); Bill McCaffery (Designer)

This book provides a thorough overview of Kazakh culture from many perspectives.

Abai and *The Path of Abai* (both undated)

by Mukhtar Auezov; L. Navrozov (Translator); H. Perham (Editor); L. Ilyina (Illustrator)

Called "Mukhtar the Great," Mukhtar Auezov was a world-renowned Kazak writer who lived from 1897 to 1961. These two epic novels are about the life and works of the founder of Kazakh literature, Abai Kunanbaev.

Kazakhstan: Coming of Age (2004)

Michael Furgus (Editor); Janar Jandosova (Contributor)

This exploration of Kazakhstan's place in the modern world traverses the country's spectacular landscape and its ecological challenges; its people and their cultures; its turbulent history and governmental structures; and the prospects for Kazakhstan's economy.

Ukraine

Geography and Population

While many people have heard of the dish Chicken Kiev, most do not know that Kiev (or Kyiv, as it is spelled in Ukraine) is named for the capital city of Ukraine. In fact there are many Ukrainian influences on mainstream society that we don't necessarily attribute to Ukraine, for it is a country just now reclaiming its national identity after years of political strife.

It seems unlikely that a country the size of Ukraine—which is the largest country in Europe after Russia—would have a difficult time preserving its national character. Bordered by great political powers like Russia and Poland, as well as Romania, Moldova, Belarus, Hungary, and Slovakia, however, Ukraine has had its hands full just trying to hold onto its independence, let alone its individuality.

Today Ukraine has the fifth-ranked population in Europe, with nearly fifty million people, 73 percent of whom are Ukrainian and 22 percent of whom are Russian. The official language is Ukrainian, an Eastern Slavonic language written in the Cyrillic script. The country is channeled with more than three thousand rivers, the largest of which is the Dnipro River. The Dnipro, which flows to the Black Sea, divides Ukraine into eastern and western regions. The western region is known for its Ukrainian nationalism, while the east bears a patina of Russian influence. The majority of people in both regions practice Ukrainian Orthodoxy.

Its many rivers make Ukraine very fertile ground for agriculture, as does its geography of rolling steppes, forests, and a few low mountain ranges. But Ukraine is also very culturally and intellectually fertile at present, with a nearly 100 percent literacy rate and an appreciation for and pride in Ukrainian literature, poetry, and art.

History and Government

The essence and tumult of Ukraine's past is encapsulated in one line of its state song, "Ukraine has not yet died." While it is true that Ukraine has not yet died, it is not for lack of other countries' trying. The country's distant history resembles a tug-of-war—with Ukraine playing the role of the rope. The heralded Cossacks, or "free men," were peasant serfs who fled to Ukraine between the fifteenth and eighteenth centuries. They set up a democracy and defended themselves against the Turks, the Poles, and the Russians. They even declared Ukraine an autonomous state. But in the eighteenth, nineteenth, and very beginning of the twentieth centuries, the rule of Ukraine passed back and forth between Poland and Russia. By 1918, Ukraine managed to proclaim its freedom, but was then absorbed into the Union of Soviet Socialist Republics (USSR).

It is estimated that in the first half of the twentieth century, half of Ukrainian men and one-quarter of the women perished due to political purges, famine, or war. Between four and ten million starved to death during the famine of 1932–1933, deliberately imposed by Joseph Stalin in response to what he perceived to be the Ukrainian people's dangerous nationalism. World War II took an additional 7.5 million lives.

With the notable exception of the 1986 accident at the nation's nuclear power plant in Chernobyl, near Kiev, the second half of the last century held more hope for Ukraine. With the collapse of the Soviet Union, Ukraine declared independence in 1991. It adopted a constitution in 1996 and currently has an elected president and legislative body, as well as an appointed prime minister.

Economy

Because of its fertile soil, Ukraine is an ideal spot for agriculture, at one point earning itself the moniker "the bread basket." The country produces a good deal of sugar, grain, sunflower seeds, sugar beets, vegetables, beef, and milk. Indeed, fields of barley, rye, wheat, and oats cover more than half of the country's land. Ukraine also has healthy deposits of coal, iron, and manganese ores. Active in the heavy metallurgical, machine-building, and chemical industries, the country trades primarily with Eastern European and Asian countries. However, Ukraine does rely heavily on imported oil and natural gases.

Ukraine was once the second most profitable republic in the USSR, after Russia. During the last decade, foreign investment in the country has increased; companies like McDonald's and Phillip Morris have proliferated, and in very recent years, Ukraine has seen modest economic and industrial growth. Nevertheless, amid political scandals, inflation, below-par transportation and communication infrastructures, and a population afflicted by poverty, the Ukrainian economy is far from steady. Many reforms are currently in the works to help stabilize and cultivate the economy.

Culture and Holidays

Dating back to 4000 B.C., the art of decorating eggs—or *pysanky*—has played prominently in Ukrainian tradition. These beautifully designed eggs began as pagan symbols used in sun worship ceremonies. They have since been adapted as Christian symbols celebrating Easter. The eggs bear diverse symbols of various meanings. For instance, a painted chicken symbolizes fertility, and a triangle—which meant air, fire, and water to the pagans—now represents the Holy Trinity to Christians.

The batik designs are created using wax dye. Some of these eggs have been elevated to works of art and are displayed in museums throughout the world. Interestingly, a group of Ukrainians living in the country's western mountains, the Hutsuls, believe these eggs represent more than works of art. They insist that the fate of the world turns on the existence of the dyed eggs. According to the Hutsuls, if the custom of egg decoration stops, a serpent that is currently chained to a cliff will overrun the world. The more pysanka, the more securely the chain contains the serpent.

Another unique and ancient Ukrainian custom, still practiced in parts of the country, is Postryzhyny. On a child's first birthday, the extended family gets together for a festive celebration. Before the meal is served, the child stands at the head of the table and each godparent takes a turn cutting her hair. Each godparent makes four cuts from different sides of the child's head and then passes the scissors to the next godparent. Once the hair is collected for safekeeping, the festivities begin.

Also fundamental to Ukrainian culture are puppet theater, folk singing, and poetry, which have their roots in oral traditions and integrate epics about the Cossacks. One of the national heroes of the country, Taras Shevchenko, was a poet and painter. He began his career writing about the Cossacks and their tribulations and successes, and then he began to write about political oppression and abuse against Ukrainians. He became quite active politically, both within and out of his works. After voicing dissent against Russian oppression in the mid-nineteenth century, he was arrested and sent to Siberia for ten years, after which he was not permitted to return to his country. One of the national holidays, Taras Shevchenko Day (March 9), honors this poet on his birthday.

Ukrainian Christmas is the most celebrated holiday in the country. It begins on Christmas Eve with Holy Supper and continues until mid-January with Malanka, which is the holiday commemorating the feast of Saint Melania and coinciding with New Year's Eve on the Julien calendar. The Holy Supper features many rituals, including covering the table with two tablecloths, one for ancestors and one for those who are still living, spreading hay under the table in memory of Christ being born in a manger, and setting an extra place at the table for those who have died. The dinner boasts twelve courses, each dedicated to one of Christ's apostles. Malanka, marking the end of Ukrainian Christmas season, is celebrated with pranks and play-acting.

The Ukrainians also celebrate the Feast of St. Nicholas in early December. They give gifts on this holiday, rather than at Christmas. Ukrainian Day commemorates the free Ukraine Republic in 1918, and Ukrainian Independence Day (August 24) represents the anniversary of Ukraine's 1991 independence from the USSR. The country also celebrates Women's Day, Labor Day, New Year's Day, and Victory Day.

Food

While the French savor, collect, and age wine, the Ukrainians are busy savoring, collecting, and aging their revered dish, *salo*—or salted pig fat. Salo is often added to stews and other dishes or eaten cold with bread. Another very popular food in Ukraine is *borshch*. This deep red, soup-like dish is indigenous to Ukraine; there are many different ways of cooking it and many different recipes, depending on the region and the occasion. *Varenyky* is another common dish. It consists of boiled dumplings filled with potatoes, sauerkraut, cheese, plums, or blueberries. *Holubtsi* are stuffed cabbage rolls filled with rice, buckwheat, and meat, and *kyshka* is sausage made of buckwheat and blood. *Nalysnyky* is the predecessor to the French crepe and includes a variety of fillings, such as stewed fruit. Chicken Kyiv (or Kiev), fried chicken filled with butter, has earned a reputation across continents.

Interesting Fact

The Ukrainians offer pysanky—the traditional decorated eggs—as meaningful gifts to each other. Superstition dictates that a girl should never give her boyfriend an egg whose design does not cover the top and bottom; if she does present him with such an egg, he will lose his hair.

Literature and Other Books

Although the centuries of strife under oppressive rule left Ukrainians unable to form a national literary tradition, the country was still able to produce writers of great beauty and expression. However, many of their works have yet to be translated. Fortunately, young writers in contemporary Ukraine are emerging into international attention with renewed energy.

Selected Poetry (1997)
by Taras Shevchenko

Often considered the William Shakespeare of Ukraine, Shevchenko and his poetry, which documents the Ukrainian people's souls and struggles, are beloved national treasures.

Fox Mykyta (1978)
by Ivan Franko; William Kurelek (Illustrator); Bohdan Melnyk (Translator)

Twenty-five tales, including elements of Ukrainian folklore, relate the adventures of the wily Fox Mykyta, who relies on his wits to outwit his enemies. Franko is a famous Ukrainian philosopher; much of his work is out of print, including two well-known books, *The Turnip Farmer* and *During Work*.

From Three Worlds: New Ukrainian Writing (1996)
Ed Hogan, Askold Melnyczuk, Michael Naydan, Mykola Riabchuk, Oksana Zabuzhko (Editors)

This is a collection of stories and poems by sixteen young Ukrainian writers that reveal the rough edges and rebellion of being young in a land of a fractured past and uncertain future.

Borderland: A Journey Through the History of Ukraine (1998)
by Anna Reid

Written by a journalist in Ukraine, this book offers a historical perspective on Ukrainians through the author's research, travel, and interviews.

Ukraine: A History (1988)
by Orest Subtelny

Used at one point as a textbook for high schools and universities, this readable book provides a detailed and comprehensive exploration of contemporary Ukraine and its history.

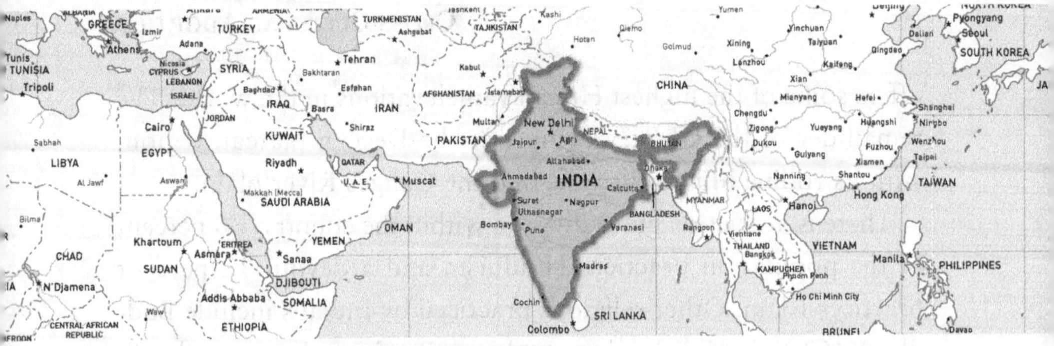

The Republic of India

Geography and Population

India houses over 15 percent of the world's population in only 2 percent of the world's land space. In other words, India has the second largest population in the world (over one billion people, second only to China) living in the seventh largest country. And to put it another way, on India's land mass, which is about one-third the size of the United States, quadruple the number of people reside. Most of this population—70 percent, to be exact—live in rural areas; only thirty percent live in urban areas like India's capital, New Delhi, and its largest city, Bombay.

In addition to Pakistan on the west and China on the north, India is bordered by Myanmar, Bangladesh, Bhutan, and Nepal, as well as the Indian Ocean, the Arabian Sea, and the Bay of Bengal. Situated in Southern Asia, the northern part of the country offers some of the highest Himalayan elevations in the world. The remainder of the country comprises the Deccan plateau region, with its rolling hills and rivers, and the Ganges River plain.

There is a strict religious division within the country: 80 percent of the population practices Hinduism and a devout 12 percent practices Islam. Other religions practiced by Indians include Buddhism, Christianity, Jainism, Sikhism, Parsis, Judaism, and folk religions. Religious division, along with border disputes with Pakistan and China, has troubled India's leaders and people for many years.

Religious division within India is equalled by its linguistic division. Hindi has been declared the official language, despite the fact that much of the country does not speak it. English has been the language of politics, scholars, and the elite, but it is not universal. Indians speak over one thousand other languages, dialects, and tongues, including Bengali, Punjabi, and Sanskrit.

History and Government

India is one of the world's oldest civilizations, dating back to 4000 B.C., with evidence of Aryan settlements and the origins of Hinduism beginning around 2000 B.C. Its relatively recent history commenced in 1526, when Muslim invaders kicked off the Mughal Empire, which endured until 1857. Around 1650, the architects and artists of that empire built the famed Taj Mahal, which was designed as a tomb for the Emperor Shah Jahan's favorite wife.

During the Mughal Empire, India began trading with the English, French, Dutch, and Portuguese. Each European country had trading posts within India, the most well-known of which was the British-owned East India Company. Behind the commercial front of the East India Company, the British began to expand their political power and territorial control over India. Claiming direct rule over India in 1858, the British empire ruled most of the country for close to a century. Many Indian rebellions and uprisings ensued, the most successful of which were those led by Mohandas K. Gandhi, a leader in the Indian independence movement by 1920. Gandhi persuaded millions of Indians to engage in "nonviolent disobedience," which included boycotting British goods, refusing to pay taxes, and rejecting British jobs, schools, courts, and government services. Gandhi's influence led to increasing recognition of Indian self-governance. After divided allegiances in World War II, and increasing violence between Hindus and Muslims, India became an independent nation on August 15, 1947, and a new country, Pakistan, was partitioned off primarily for Muslims. The separation spurred the largest mass exodus in history; over ten million people became refugees, as Hindus and Sikhs in Pakistan fled to India, and Muslims in India fled to Pakistan. About half a million people were killed in the accompanying riots, including Gandhi, who was assassinated by a Hindu fanatic who hated him for his teachings of tolerance.

Jawaharlal Nehru began his relatively stable rule of India in 1949. That same year, Indian leaders developed and signed a constitution marking the birth of the world's largest democracy. After Nehru's death, his daughter Indira Gandhi eventually became prime minister and continued his policies, ruling (not without opposition) until 1984 when Sikh militants assassinated her. Her son, Rajiv Gandhi, took over, but he too was assassinated in 1991.

In 1996, India entered a series of coalition governments. Today, the government—which is a federal republic with a parliament, president, and prime minister—is implementing wide economic reforms, expanding trade, and encouraging foreign investment. India's constitution, which has remained in force since 1950, guarantees equal rights to all citizens and prohibits discrimination on the basis of race, sex, caste (social class), religion, or place of birth.

Economy

India has enormous economic potential with its stores of untapped natural and human resources, the fourth largest coal reserves in the world, and plentiful cattle. India produces enough agricultural products—including rice, cotton, wheat, jute, sugar cane, and tea, as well as opium used in pharmaceuticals (and illegally)—to support much of its population. India consistently reports the highest worldwide student test scores for math and science and produces more engineers than any other country in the world. In fact, India's epic economic plight seems quite distant in the highly industrialized cities, where India has become the largest exporter of cut diamonds, boasts the most prolific film business in the world, has developed a thriving textile industry, and fertilizes emerging electronics, software, and engineering enterprises.

Yet many of the natural resources remain unexploited because of economic shortages. And the cattle are of limited value because of the Hindu religious prohibition against slaughter. Moreover, the caste system prevents economic mobility for large segments of the population. So despite established and growing industry, a myriad of resources, and the fact that agriculture is India's largest industry, over 40 percent of the population is too poor to purchase adequate food on a regular basis.

Culture and Holidays

To the outsider, India buzzes with the exotic, from its moody sitar music to its lively festivals, spicy food, glittering textiles, multi-god religion, arranged marriages, and old-world caste system.

Hinduism and the caste system dominate social order and control Indian society. Castes represent social levels, often defined by occupation, that dictate a person's or family's place in Indian society. Family of birth determines social level or caste, and it is difficult, if not impossible, to move into a different caste by virtue of performance or marriage; only through reincarnation can caste membership improve. Some of the castes include rulers or clergy, while others are composed of merchants, military men, farmers, or servants. But occupation just hits the surface level of the meaning of belonging to a particular caste, and while Indian laws have softened the once-stricter occupational barriers between castes, the social barriers separating castes remain solidly in place. A large group of people—about 15 percent of the population—is considered to be outside the caste system. Known as "untouchables" or *dalit* (downtrodden), this group has traditionally held the most undesirable jobs, such as cleaning toilets and disposing of garbage. Although the Indian Constitution guarantees this group equal rights and forbids discrimination, and the Indian government has set aside government jobs, scholarships, and legislative seats for them, the concept of the "untouchable" persists in Indian society.

Hinduism and the caste system are linked in part because Hinduism teaches that good acts in life can improve caste position in the next life. Beyond reincarnation, Hindus believe in a single spiritual force—God, also called Brahman—who takes many forms. These are the many gods and goddesses of Hindu belief, including Vishnu, Shiva, and Ganesh, and Hindus worship whichever forms suit them. Hindus celebrate many festivals, including Diwali in the fall and Holi, which marks the arrival of spring. During Holi, people sprinkle colored water and powders on each other. The colors symbolize the exuberance and vibrancy of the season.

An introduction to Indian culture would be incomplete without a mention of arranged marriage, which, despite modernization in many other areas, remains the method by which most marriages form in India. Within the constraints of the caste system, "aunts" organize a complex schedule of meetings and interviews in order to complete a family match. Often these matches involve dowries. Although historically India has enjoyed a far lower divorce rate than the United States, the divorce rate has been climbing in recent years.

Food

The mention of Indian cuisine brings to mind the aroma of spices, exotic flavors, and ocherous shades of yellow and orange. The country's food has become one of the favorite "ethnic" foods in America and is the UK's equivalent to "ordering a pizza." There is more to Indian food, however, than meets the stomach, so to speak, for even their food is imbued with religious underpinnings. Not only are a good number of Hindus vegetarians (the cow is sacred), but when creating Indian cuisine, each ingredient is considered to have a specific physical and/or spiritual benefit. Ingredients in any given dish are based on six flavors, which correspond to their specific benefits: sour, pungent, salty, sweet, astringent, and bitter.

Divided regionally, cuisine in the north of the country involves more meat and bread, while the southerners eat more rice, spicy curry, and vegetarian dishes. In the south, the people do not use utensils to eat; instead, they scoop up the food with their right hands.

Indian food is renowned for its use of curry and for being cooked in a tandoor, which is a clay, coal oven. Tandoori meats are juicy and tender. Darjeeling tea is a popular Indian drink and export.

Interesting Fact

India is the only country that has a Bill of Rights dedicated to cows.

Literature and Other Books for Further Reading

Indian literature is prolific, award-winning, and diverse. Written by Indian natives in a variety of languages ranging from Sanskrit to English, books like the *Kama Sutra* and the world's longest epic, *The Mahabharata*, have become internationally renowned. The following list represents just a tiny sampling of the impressive national collection.

Clear Light of Day (1980)
by Anita Desai

This novel tells the bittersweet story of a contemporary Indian woman who confronts familial pain and devotion. Set in India's Old Delhi, it explores religious division between Muslims and Hindus and political issues after the death of Gandhi.

The God of Small Things (1997)
by Arundhati Roy

This award-winning novel narrates the life and struggles of a Christian family in 1960s Kerala, a small state in India.

Interpreter of Maladies—Stories of Bengal, Boston and Beyond (1999)
by Jhumpa Lahiri

Lahiri spins her tales, some set in India and others in the United States, of Indian customs and heritage into a Pulitzer Prize–winning collection.

Midnight's Children (1981)
by Salman Rushdie

Native son Salman Rushdie wrote this 1980 Booker Prize–winning allegorical story about two children, sons of a Hindu family and a wealthy Muslim family, who are switched at birth at the moment at which India became an independent nation.

A Fine Balance (1996)

by Rohinton Mistry

Set in India of the 1970s, amid political strife, economic troubles, and sterilization campaigns, this notable novel tells the story of four individuals struggling to survive.

Panchatantra (undated)

These Aesop's fable–like tales are written in five volumes—"Loss of Friends," "Winning of Friends," "Crows and Owls," "Loss of Gains," and "Ill-Considered Action"—and read to children throughout India. They are incorporated into many different books available in English translation.

The Socialist Republic of Vietnam

Geography and Population

Vietnam is a quilt of rice paddies dotted with women wearing conical hats (called *non la*). Bordered by China to the north and Laos and Cambodia to the west, Vietnam has coastlines along the South China Sea, the Gulf of Tonkin, and the Gulf of Thailand. The northern part of the S-shaped country is a densely populated region that includes the capital city of Hanoi, as well as the agriculturally fertile Red River Delta. Central Vietnam is mountainous and more sparsely populated. The south is dominated by the agricultural patchwork of the Mekong River Delta—also known as the "rice bowl" of Vietnam. Ho Chi Minh City (formerly named Saigon) is the southern region's largest city and the country's economic hub.

Covering roughly the same land mass as the state of New Mexico, Vietnam has eighty million people. Over 85 percent are ethnic Vietnamese—called Kinh—and the remaining minority consists of more than fifty ethnic groups, including the Tay, Tai, Hmong, and Khmer. Most Vietnamese live in rural villages, and most are farmers whose lives are structured around the cultivation of crops, especially rice.

The national language is Vietnamese, which is rooted in Chinese. In urban areas, English is the most widely spoken foreign language, but Chinese, French, and Russian are also spoken.

History and Government

The Vietnamese Communist party, which is the only party in Vietnam, rules Vietnam's unitary system of government. Today, exclusive power lies with this central, national government. But the Communist Party did not come by its power easily.

The history of Vietnam, like that of most Asian countries, is long and vast. The country has been populated by fascinating civilizations and kingdoms since prehistoric times. The centuries of Chinese occupation from 111 B.C. to 939 A.D. left Vietnam forever infused with Chinese influences. Vietnam remained relatively independent through several long-lasting dynasties, including the Ly and the Tran dynasties, until the French arrived in 1858. The French conquered Vietnam, Cambodia, and Laos and called its new colony Indochina.

Vietnam remained a French colony until the twentieth century, when Vietnam's nationalist movement began to collect fervor. During World War II, the Japanese overthrew the French government in Indochina. The Vietnamese, led by Ho Chi Minh and other leaders of the Indochinese Communist Party, formed an organization called the Vietminh, designed to encourage national unity and independence. After Japan's surrender in 1945, the Vietminh staged a revolution, with Ho Chi Minh declaring Vietnam's independence (he quoted directly from the American Declaration of Independence).

But France wanted its colony back, and the two countries began a deadly war, which lasted from 1946 until 1954. Many southern Vietnamese, fearing the Communist government of the Vietminh, sided with the French.

The war ended with the Geneva Accords. One of these agreements temporarily divided Vietnam into northern and southern contingents. Another agreement called for an election to unify the country, but fearing that Ho Chi Minh would win, southern Vietnam, with United States support, refused to participate, and the election was never held.

The Vietnam War—which the Vietnamese call the American War—began in 1957. Communist-supported rebels in the South, called the Viet Cong, revolted against the southern Vietnamese government, which was backed by the United States. The revolt soon turned into a full-fledged war. The United States sent troops and became heavily involved economically and militarily. Throughout the more than ten years of war, Vietnam sustained enormous damage, especially in the rural areas. Missions like the Tet Offensive of 1968 destroyed entire regions and killed thousands. By 1969, public pressure in the United States had mounted to such an extent that the United States began to withdraw some of its 550,000 troops. Nevertheless, the fighting continued.

In 1973, a cease-fire allowed the north to begin reconstruction, but fighting continued in the south. But by 1975, the south could no longer sustain its defense. The troops withdrew, the president resigned, and the north came in and took over without any opposition. Vietnam became a unified country under a single Communist government by the next year. More than one million southern Vietnamese either fled the country (settling in the United States, Canada, Australia, Belgium, and France) or were subjected to "reeducation" in the political culture of the north, which often included forced labor and torture.

But peace was short-lived in Vietnam. In 1978, Vietnam invaded Cambodia, replacing Cambodia's Khmer Rouge Communist government with a pro-Vietnamese Communist government. The fighting lasted until 1991.

Vietnam has found peace at last in the years since 1989. As part of the Vietnamese government's postwar economic restructuring, known as *doi moi*, Vietnam encouraged private enterprise and foreign trade and investment. In July 1995, Vietnam and the United States established diplomatic ties, and, in July 2000, the two countries signed a trade agreement, clearing the way for normal trade relations.

Economy

After the war ended, Vietnam experienced an economic boom. Agriculture is the country's leading industry and, since its two river deltas are some of the best places to grow rice in the entire world, rice is its main crop. Vietnam's other chief exports include coffee, tea, petroleum, rubber, clothing and textiles, and fish and shellfish. Its primary trading partners are Japan, Singapore, South Korea, and Taiwan.

Industry in Vietnam, once hampered by the lengthy war, has also begun to take off. The country has made significant progress in recent years in the agricultural-processing, machine-building, automobile-assembly, and tourist industries. Its highly literate population, educated in public schools that emphasize Communist ideology and technology, may assist Vietnam to become, as some economists predict, the next Asian economic giant.

Culture and Holidays

Although the ravages of war have left Vietnam struggling financially, the country has managed to remain quite rich in culture, social morals, crafts, and traditions. Vietnam reflects—and indeed takes advantage of—its dual Asian and French influences, thereby making the proverbial lemonade out of colonial lemons. Chinese heritage and French culture not only infuse Vietnamese religion and art but have also contributed to the country's air of tolerance.

A unique religious tolerance pervades sectarian Vietnam. While the country has a small number of Christians and Muslims, most Vietnamese practice a religion known as Tam Gao (also known as the Triple Religion or Three Teachings), which is a melding of Taoism, Confucianism, and Mahayana Buddhism, with a touch of ancient Vietnamese animism (the worship of animals, plants, and nature). Perhaps this spiritual mélange is a recipe for religious tolerance because, historically, Vietnam is one of the few countries that cannot claim religion as a source of disharmony.

Vietnam is also united in its social code. Confucianism dictates that family is of primary importance, particularly respect for elders. The Vietnamese prioritize family over all other values, and special emphasis is placed on honoring the dead. The Cult of Ancestors is a set of beliefs and practices designed to show respect for, and avoid offense to, ancestors, and it is manifested in most Vietnamese homes with a family altar. Altars can be rudimentary or lavish, but they all symbolize the same thing: a peaceful place to honor ancestors.

The idea of death is rarely a depressing one in Vietnamese culture; after all, dead ancestors, so spiritually alive, are the most elevated people in Vietnamese society. Two festivals in their honor take place during the year: Trung Nguyen (or Wandering Souls Day) and Thanh Minh. On Trung Nguyen, which takes place in August, Vietnamese throw huge festivals where they offer gifts and food to the souls of the forgotten dead. Thanh Minh, celebrated in early spring, is the holiday on which the Vietnamese visit and weed the tombs of their deceased relatives.

But not all of the many Vietnamese festivals celebrate the dead. The biggest festival, Tet (unfortunately made into a household name because of the military initiative of the same moniker) celebrates the new year. The Vietnamese decorate their homes with peach blossoms to ward off evil spirits and light fireworks at midnight to usher in the new year. Tet Trung Thu (or Mid-Autumn Moon Festival) is another popular celebration in Vietnam. Started as a way for parents to turn attention back to their children after the long harvest season, it has morphed into an extended holiday for children. Costumed kids parade in the streets, carrying handmade, brightly colored lanterns, and families exchange traditional mooncakes.

Vietnam absorbed Chinese and French art, but then created its own unique style of arts and crafts. Brightly colored weavings made on wooden looms, blue and white ceramics, and wooden water puppets represent some of the more popular types of Vietnamese crafts. Vietnamese silk paintings have also earned international acclaim. Many of these paintings include images of flowers, which are very important in Vietnamese culture—so important, in fact, that many of the most popular girls' names (such as Lan, Mai, and Hue) are names of flowers.

Food

The Vietnamese chew betel and areca nuts as a part of their tradition. In fact, every wedding and special occasion must feature a dish of these nuts. Sharing betel symbolizes camaraderie, like sharing drinks in other cultures. Aside from—and perhaps resulting in—its cultural importance, betel is said to make the mouth smell good, aid with digestion, and alleviate bad moods.

Tea, usually green, also plays prominently in Vietnamese culture. Its preparation, serving, and drinking etiquette possess social importance. For instance, while servants in Vietnam serve liquor, the actual host will always serve the tea. When tea is steeping, it is important to keep the tea, the teapot, and the teacups as the main topic of conversation. Moreover, the Vietnamese believe it uncouth to drink the last drop in the teacup because it contains tea leaves, which are the "dregs" of the tea. The tea-sharing ritual takes place before conducting business, participating in religious or scholarly ceremonies, or engaging in romantic encounters. The Vietnamese drink hot tea day and night, winter and summer.

Aside from tea, rice is the staple in Vietnam. Other common foods include *cha gio,* or spring rolls; *nuoc mam,* fermented fish sauce used for dipping; and *pho,* noodle soup with fresh vegetables and meat or seafood. Eel soup, exotic meats, and unusual fruit, such as dragon fruit, pomels, and three-seed cherries, also feature in Vietnamese cuisine.

Interesting Fact

In light of the Vietnamese preoccupation with ancestors, it is not surprising that many Vietnamese families still follow an ancient custom prescribing second burials for the dead. Second burials, or happy burials, take place three years after a death, at night, at a time preordained by a fortune-teller. A "happy gravedigger," as are nicknamed these professionals (they must complete training through a one-year apprenticeship before becoming qualified to perform this ritual), accompanies the family to the original site of the tomb. While the family chants prayers and burns incense, the gravedigger unearths the bones from the grave and burns the remaining clothing. The family then follows the gravedigger to a special set of sinks where he cleans the bones, wraps them gingerly in tissue paper, and stacks them in a ceramic box. The gravedigger stacks the bones in an order that corresponds to the human skeleton, and in a manner that ensures the most comfort for the deceased person. After sealing the box, the family members carry it to their home village and rebury it there.

Literature and Other Books for Further Reading

Although the Vietnamese government controls all newspapers, magazines, and television and radio broadcasts, Vietnamese authors have still found beautiful ways of expressing themselves. Vietnamese literature has been shaped by its proximity to China. Like Chinese, it too is a culture replete with legends and folklore. Often these legends explain phenomena like the weather or traits like greed. Interestingly, Vietnamese writings explore similar themes but reach different conclusions than those of the Chinese. The following is a sampling of writings about Vietnam and/or by Vietnamese authors.

The Tale of Kieu (1973)

by Nguyen Du; Annotated by Hu`ynh Sanh Thong (Translator)

This epic poem, written in the early 1800s, is considered a Vietnamese masterpiece. The characters in its love story and social commentary have become so well-known that lines and ideas from the poem have entered mainstream vernacular throughout the country.

The Stone Boy and Other Stories (1996)

by Thich Nhat Hanh

These fictional short stories, written by a Zen Buddhist monk living in France, explore themes of love and compassion set deep in Vietnamese culture.

The House on Dream Street: Memoir of an American Woman in Vietnam (2000)

by Dana Sachs

This is the Vietnamese equivalent to Peter Mayles' *A Year in Provence*. An American ex-patriot tells of her extended stay and experiences in Vietnam.

The Sorrow of War (1995)
by Bao Ninh; Frank Palmos (Editor); Phan Thanh Hao (Translator)

Like *Gone With the Wind*, Bao Ninh's haunting literary novel about lost innocence contrasts the beauty of Vietnamese life before the war with the sorrow and destruction of the postwar country.

Sweet Dried Apples: A Vietnamese Wartime Childhood (1996)
by Rosemary Breckler, Deborah Kogan Ray (Illustrator)

This children's book features a touching story about a girl in Vietnam during the war.

Paradise of the Blind: A Novel (1993)
by Duong Thu Huong; Phan Huy Duong and Nina McPherson (Translators)

Well-known writer Duong Thu Huong, who lives with her children in Hanoi, depicts the complexity of Vietnamese culture—the allegiance to family and ancestors, the symbolic value of food, class distinctions, and the continuing sense of desperation mingled with pride.

The Republic of Colombia

Geography and Population

Colombia is a large South American country, perhaps best known worldwide by two names—Juan Valdez and Gabriel Garciá Marquez. Aside from coffee and literature, though, Colombia possesses a rich cultural and ethnic heritage that has carried its people through generations of strife. Colombians, now numbering approximately forty-two million, are of various ancestries, including *mestizo*, a mix of indigenous tribe and European; *mulatto*, a mix of European and African; European; and Indian. The population has grown to its present size from just twelve million in the middle of the twentieth century because, until the 1960s, the fertility rate averaged seven children per woman. The rate has since declined.

Colombia is sizable enough and, it would seem, homogenous enough to house its large population with relative peace. The country is the size of Texas, New Mexico, and Arkansas combined.

Nearly all of its people speak Spanish, although there are over 175 languages that indigenous tribes speak in addition to Spanish. And 90 percent of the population practices Roman Catholicism. Most of the people live in the lowland valley cities that gaze up at one of three western Andean mountain ranges. Many live in and outside of Bogotá, the capital.

More sparsely populated, the eastern part of Colombia is covered by jungle, and the remainder of the country lies on coastal lowlands. The equator crosses southern Colombia. Powerful neighbors—Panama, Venezuela, Ecuador, Peru, and Brazil—press in on Colombia. But they do not surround the country completely; Colombia is in the unique position to boast both an Atlantic and Pacific Ocean coastline.

History and Government

Despite its beautiful setting and its relative homogeneity of language, religion, and ethnicity, Colombia's history and present are marred by acrimony. The recent history of the region began in the 1500s when the Spanish arrived and conquered the native Indians. The Spaniards incorporated what is now Colombia into Peru. Colombia remained part of Peru for two hundred years, until 1739 when the Spanish created New Granada, a super-nation of the countries that are today known as Colombia, Venezuela, Ecuador, and Panama. It was not until 1819 that Colombia broke free from New Granada and formed its own republic. The name Colombia was chosen to honor the Italian navigator, Christopher Columbus.

By the time Colombia became a republic, the two political foes that still dominate Colombian politics had formed. These forces, the centralist Conservative Party and the federalist Liberal Party, kicked off eight civil wars that would consume Colombia's nineteenth century (during which eight different constitutions were written). These civil wars culminated in 1899's War of a Thousand Days, which led to the death of 100,000 people.

Colombia's twentieth century suffered similar instability. Periods of military power traded off and overlapped with periods of political struggle between the parties. In 1948, this political instability, along with the assassination of popular Liberal Party leader Jorge Eliecer Gaitan, led to a series of riots over a period of almost twenty years called La Violencia, in which more than 200,000 died. After La Violencia, the two warring parties formed a coalition government called the National Front, which lasted until 1974.

Complicating matters, Communist guerillas, drug traffickers, and right-wing paramilitary groups became head-turning presences in the twentieth century, threatening the shaky government stability even further. Drug trafficking, especially cocaine, is big business in Colombia, and the large drug cartels often wield more power than political or governmental figures. The cartels secure and enhance this power by sending out death squads to quiet any groups opposing them. Despite a joint effort with the United States to weaken the drug trade, recent arrests of key drug figures, and a new constitution in 1991 strengthening governmental control and revising the criminal code, violent civil war continues to plague Colombia today.

Economy

With a twelve-month growing season, close economic ties to the United States, and a free market, the Colombian economy has grown significantly in the twentieth century. The country's most famous agricultural product is coffee; about ten percent of the world's trade in coffee comes from Colombia. Other major crops include flowers, bananas, rice, corn, sugar cane, and cocoa beans. Colombia is a leading exporter of petroleum and hydropower, and also has healthy deposits of natural gas, coal, iron, nickel, gold, copper, and platinum.

Colombia even provides half of the world's emerald supply. Industry, such as textile, food processing, oil, clothes, and chemicals, continues to grow.

Until a 1999 recession, Colombia savored notable economic growth compared to other Latin American countries. The recession, due in large part to the violent conditions, yielded inflation and unemployment, from which the country is now recovering.

Culture and Holidays

Colombians take pride in the artists that they have launched to international renown. The beloved Gabriel Garciá Marquez, best known for his mystical storytelling in *One Hundred Years of Solitude* and *Love in the Time of Cholera*, won the Nobel Prize for literature. The artist Fernando Botero became famous for his quirky but elegant works of people and objects with bloated, exaggerated proportions. His paintings and other works are exhibited in museums around the world, and several of his sculptures line the Champs Élysées in Paris. The musician Shakira, the actor John Leguizamo, and Formula One racecar champion Juan Montoya are all of Colombian descent.

While proud of its world-famous artists and athletes, Colombia has recognized the importance of education at home and has taken a unique approach to achieving its high literacy rate of 91 percent. Colombian law dictates that all employers earning over a certain amount and located more than two kilometers from a school must establish a primary school for children of company employees. This proliferation and privatization of schools has made it easier for parents to take children to school and for the schools to maintain higher educational standards.

The Colombian passion for art and education is equaled by its pious devotion to Catholicism. A fusion of Indian, Spanish, and

African traditions has made its way into celebrations of traditional Catholic holidays. In the streets during the Holy Week of Easter, the country reenacts Christ's crucifixion and resurrection, complete with traditional costumes. The country likewise celebrates its own national holidays like Columbus Day (October 12), which is also known as Day of the Race or Native American Day.

Food

Colombian coffee—symbolized by Juan Valdez, the trademark of the National Federation of Coffee Growers of Colombia—has become ubiquitous both in and out of Colombia. One is hard-pressed to find a coffeehouse in the United States that does not blend some type of Colombian roast, but Colombians do not drink as much coffee as Americans and Europeans do. Both adults and children drink *agua de panela,* a beverage consisting of brown sugar dissolved in water. Colombian fare features chicken, pork, rice, beans, and potatoes. A typical meal may include *ajiaco,* a soup made with chicken and potatoes; empanadas; and fried plantains. Colombians also enjoy a dish called *lechona*, which is suckling pig roasted on a spit and stuffed with rice. At certain times of year, Colombians enjoy an age-old delicacy called *hormiga culona*, or toasted big-bottomed ants. The Colombians sell this delicacy, used originally by indigenous tribes to treat stomach complaints, on roadside stands. The ants reportedly taste like popcorn and possess aphrodisiac effects.

Interesting Fact

One of Colombia's most popular places of worship has quite a unique characteristic: It is made entirely of salt. The Cathedral of Salt, located in Zipaquira, Colombia, in a salt mine 390 feet underground, is made of 250,000 tons of salt and took five years to build.

Literature and Other Books for Further Reading

Colombians love their writers, especially poets. Although many works that are famous in Latin American countries, such as *Maria*, a novel written in 1867 by Jorge Isaacs, and the beloved poetry of Alvaro Mutis, have not been translated into English, Colombia has inspired much literature, poetry, folklore, and political commentary in recent history. The following is a sampling of some of the best-known books.

Love in the Time of Cholera (1988)
by Gabriel Garciá Marquez; Edith Grossman (Translator)

This is the famous mystical love story from a Nobel laureate and Colombian native.

Living to Tell the Tale (2003)
by Gabriel Garciá Marquez; Edith Grossman (Translator)

This long-awaited memoir is the first of three projected volumes on the famous writer's life. Peopled with unforgettable characters and drawn from pivotal events in Colombia's history, this book captures the myth, mysteries, brutality, and beauty of Colombia through Garciá's uniquely observant eyes.

Until Death Do Us Part: My Struggle to Reclaim Colombia (2002)
by Ingrid Betancourt; Steven Rendall (Translator)

This memoir, written by a Colombian senator and presidential candidate, recounts a personal and political struggle against the legitimate governmental establishment and the power of the illegal drug lords

Colombia: Fragmented Land, Divided Society (Latin American Histories) (2001)
by Frank Safford and Marco Palacios

This work is considered to be a key resource on the history and politics of Colombia. It explores the relationship of politics to drugs and the United States' role in current Colombian affairs.

The Monkey People: A Colombian Folktale (1995)
by Eric Metaxas; Diana Bryan (Illustrator); Raul Julia (Narrator)

For children ages five to nine, this book-and-cassette interpretation of a traditional Colombian folktale tells the story of a tribe of people and what happens when they go to great lengths to avoid doing their chores.

The Republic of Haiti

Geography and Population

The name Haiti—which means "land of mountains"—originates from its geography. This primarily mountainous country, about the size of Maryland, is the most densely populated in Latin America. Surrounded by the Atlantic Ocean, the Caribbean Sea, the Dominican Republic, Jamaica, and Cuba, Haiti occupies the western third of the island of Hispaniola and is part of a group of islands called the West Indies. The increasingly populated capital of Haiti is Port-au-Prince, where young Haitians are migrating in search of better employment opportunities.

Haiti's population is approaching eight million. Ninety-five percent of these eight million citizens descend from West African slaves. Nonetheless, a mulatto minority (5 percent) rules the country and controls the majority of its wealth. Because of extreme poverty, political instability, and racial tension, over two million Haitians have migrated to North America.

The official language of Haiti is French, a telling detail. The mulattos speak French, while the Haitian majority speaks Haitian Creole.

History and Government

While well-publicized political turmoil reigns in Haiti today, the country recently passed its bicentennial anniversary, during which it proudly celebrated 200 years of independence and its position as the first black republic. This independence was not easily achieved, however.

Haiti's native inhabitants, the Arawak Amerindians, left their mark when they named their "land of mountains" Haiti. But Europe has left a darker stain on the country. In 1492, Christopher Columbus claimed the land for Spain. Spain overlooked the land that is now Haiti and focused its efforts on the portion of the island that is now the Dominican Republic. The French moved in to take advantage of Spain's neglect and grab up what later became known as the "Pearl of the Antilles." Using African slaves that it had shipped in, France began to deforest Haiti and develop sugar plantations. France would ultimately ship in over 500,000 West Africans to labor as slaves, producing the sugar, rum, and coffee that would render Haiti a key ingredient in enriching the French empire.

French rule officially began in 1697; during the colonization Haiti was called St. Dominique. By the late eighteenth and early nineteenth centuries, the Haitians began to stage a revolt against French rule. After a thirteen-year rebellion against Napoleon, led by black general Toussaint L'Ouverture and later by Jean Jacques Dessalines, Haiti finally achieved independence in 1804. This massive revolt remains one of the most successful slave revolts in history.

The Haitians expelled the French and Creole people from the country, leaving a society divided between blacks and mulattos. The lengthy revolt and period of colonization left not only a racially divided society, but also a severely damaged economy and a ravaged environment. After achieving independence, the country endured rule by a series of emperors until 1859, when it became a republic. Still, the political and social conflict, especially between blacks and mulattos, continued to escalate.

Fearing Haiti's instability and its potential effect on United States investments there, Americans occupied Haiti in 1915, dissolved the congress, and put in place a new constitution. Haiti resisted this intrusion, but United States troops remained in Haiti until 1934, when the Haitian armed forces were mobilized to maintain order.

After World War II, political instability continued, corruption plagued the government, and military coup attempts were frequent and violent. Francois Duvalier became dictator and declared himself "president for life." He formed a paramilitary group called the Tonton Macoutes and, during his rule, hundreds of thousands of Haitians perished. His 1971 death put an end to his own lifetime presidency, but his son, who held to similar policies, succeeded him. Duvalier's son, nicknamed "Baby Doc," ruled until 1986, when the family was exiled, with U.S. assistance.

Although 1991 brought the first free elections and elected president, Jean-Bertrand Aristide, the army soon took control of the country and forced him to flee. The United Nations stepped in, imposed a trade embargo, and threatened military action unless the country reinstated the president. That same year, 38,000 "boat people" attempted to emigrate to the United States.

Political turmoil continues to plague Haiti today and is frequently (and unfortunately) a subject of international news.

Economy

Part of the reason for the political instability is an inability to resolve Haiti's dire economic straits. A few simple statistics illuminate Haiti's economic position. Half of the Haitian population is unemployed. Three-quarters of the population lives in what is considered to be extreme poverty. And Haiti has been rated the poorest country in the Western Hemisphere.

Those Haitians who are employed toil primarily as subsistence farmers. These farmers generally live in one-room shacks, with no electricity or running water. They cultivate beans and sweet potatoes by using picks and hoes. The Haitians have planted on every conceivable piece of land, sometimes having to use ropes to climb up to cultivate crops planted on ground that is too steep to reach otherwise.

Haiti does engage in some trade; it is mostly with the United States and includes some light manufacturing, as well as cassava, rice, sugarcane, yams, corn, and plantains. Haiti also possesses some natural resources, like gold and copper, but most of these resources remain untapped. Once a plentiful natural resource, the trees of Haiti have been almost completely eliminated. Vast deforestation, along with overpopulation—the population continues to grow, even as the economy shrinks—have led to severe environmental degradation.

Tourism, which is profitable for many of the other Caribbean countries, is not a boon on which Haiti can rely. Aside from its political and social instability, its overburdened infrastructure, and its poverty, Haiti also boasts some of the highest death rates from AIDS in the world. The epidemic in Haiti has earned it, whether deserved or not, an international reputation as a hotbed for the virus.

Culture and Holidays

Voodoo—or Vodoun, as it is correctly spelled—thoroughly pervades Haitian social, cultural, and religious life. Although many Haitians practice Roman Catholicism as their mainstay religion, almost all Haitians also practice or weave in Vodoun to some extent. Vodoun infiltrates all aspects of Haitian society, to the point where Haitians consult Vodoun priests for everything from religious matters to sickness, fertility issues to politics and social disputes.

The African slaves brought Vodoun to Haiti. It combines the worship of African nature gods with rituals honoring spirits through dances, drumming, spirit possessions, food offerings, and animal sacrifices. Prayer includes performing rites to please the deities, like creating colorful prayer flags. These vibrant flags, like many other types of Haitian folk art, are collected and displayed internationally.

The Haitians are known not only for their art, but also for their love of music and dance. The meringue is the national dance, and Haitian music includes American jazz and Cuban influences, as well as zook, which meshes French and African rhythms. Dancing and music play prominently in Vodoun rituals and celebrations.

One of the largest Vodoun celebrations is called Rara. It takes place during Lent and features bands wending their way around the country, playing drums and handmade wind instruments, singing songs, and encouraging onlookers to dance. Rara begins just after Carnival, which is one of the country's most festive celebrations. A unique feature of Haitian Carnival is the fact that walking bands play music with made-up lyrics poking fun at local politics. They draw crowds as they go.

The Haitians have an interesting way of celebrating both All Saints Day and All Souls Day. In the Vodoun tradition, practitioners roam cemeteries and neighborhoods dressed as deceased people or undertakers. These individuals dance with other "dead people" they meet during their stroll.

Aside from Vodoun, Haiti's brightly colored and internationally acclaimed folk art, and the country's love of music and dance, the

Haitian sense of humor also characterizes Haiti's culture. Perhaps the Haitians have needed to rely on their sense of humor to sweeten their difficult circumstances. Haiti boasts such a rich oral tradition that storytelling and riddle-telling have become a form of performance art. Storytellers pride themselves on the different voices they use to portray different characters in their stories. Performers gauge whether their audience is ready for a story by shouting out "Krik!" When the audience responds "Krak!" the storyteller knows that it is time to begin.

Food

Though it is little known on a universal scale, Haitian nationals pride themselves on their cuisine. With a combination of Caribbean, French, and African influences, Haitian cuisine fuses balance and flavor with color and variety. Rice and kidney beans (or *riz et pois*) is the national dish and staple. Chicken and goat are the most popular meats. Red snapper and cod are the main catches and are served whole, smoked, or salted. Many dishes are peppered with dried black mushrooms called *djon-djon* that are said to grow only in Haiti. A typical Haitian meal will often include pumpkin soup, pressed plantains, conch, spicy Creole sauces, and lots of shellfish, tropical fruits and vegetables, starches like polenta, and root vegetables like yucca.

Interesting Fact

Haitians ingest more chicken and goat than they do other meats, such as pork. The reason for this preference is that chickens eat chicken feed and goats live on grass and leaves. Pigs, on the other hand, compete with humans for food. Where food is in short supply, as it is in Haiti, people cannot raise animals that need to eat food that could be nourishment for themselves and their families.

Literature and Other Books for Further Reading

Krik? Krak! (1995)
by Edwidge Danticat

Written by critically acclaimed Haitian-American author Danticat, this collection of nine powerful stories tells about life under Haiti's dictatorships: the terrorism of the Tonton Macoutes; the slaughtering of hope and the resiliency of love; those who fled to America to give their children a better life and those who stayed behind in the villages; and the linkages of generations of women through the magical tradition of storytelling.

Papa Toussaint (1998)
by C. Richard Gillespie

This historical novel chronicles the revolutionary role of former slave Toussaint Louverture, who fought for racial equality in Haiti. The novel opens in 1816 and is narrated by Toussaint's son, Placide, exiled in France.

Song of Haiti (2000)
by Barry Paris

This is the inspiring tale of Larimer Mellon, son of ultra-wealthy financier William L. Mellon, who went to medical school in his forties. After medical school, Mellon and his wife, Gwen, a medical lab technician, left their comfortable Arizona ranch and moved to poverty-stricken Haiti. In the Artibonite Valley, where life expectancy was the lowest in the hemisphere, they built the Albert Schweitzer Hospital. Larry Mellon served as a physician there for the rest of his life. Gwen Mellon, now in her eighties, still lives in Haiti and works for the hospital.

Haiti in Focus: A Guide to the People, Politics, and Culture (In Focus Guides) (2002)
by Charles Arthur

This authoritative and up-to-date guide explores the land of Haiti, its history and politics, economy, society and people, culture, and environment.

Tap-Tap (1994)
by Karen Lynn Williams; Catherine Stock (Illustrator)

This colorfully illustrated children's book tells the story of a young girl, Sasifi, and her first market day with her mother, where she becomes entranced by the tap-tap, a covered, festively painted pickup truck carrying marketgoers and their goods.

The Magic Orange Tree: and Other Haitian Folktales (1997)
by Diane Wolkstein

A magical collection of Haitian folktales for readers of all ages.

Resources for Learning More about Adoption

In addition to your bookstore and library shelves, the Internet connects you to hundreds of resources for learning more about cross-cultural adoption. Here are just a few:

Organizations for Adoption Research, Advocacy, and Education

AdoptiveFamilies.Com
www.adoptivefamilies.com

Publishes *Adoptive Families*, the award-winning national adoption magazine. Its website is a treasure-trove of adoption information.

Evan B. Donaldson Adoption Institute
20 Wall Street, 20th Floor
New York, NY 10005
212.269.5080
www.adoptioninstitute.org

Through research, education, advocacy, and innovative programs, the Evan P. Donaldson Adoption Institute has set the standard for improving adoption awareness and understanding. On its website is a wealth of resources for those interested in adoption issues.

Institute for Adoption Information
P.O. Box 4405
Bennington, VT 05201
www.adoptioninformationinstitute.org

The Institute for Adoption Information is a nonprofit organization dedicated to increasing awareness of adoption issues, using positive adoption language and concepts in everyday life, and advocating for balanced, accurate coverage of adoption in news and entertainment media. The organization offers on its website the excellent resources: "An Educator's Guide to Adoption" and "A Journalist's Guide to Adoption."

Joint Council on International Children's Services
1403 King Street, Suite 101
Alexandria, VA 22314
703.535.8045
www.jcics.org

Umbrella organization of licensed, non-profit international adoption agencies. Members include adoption agencies, child welfare organizations, parent support groups, and medical specialists with an interest in intercountry adoptions.

National Adoption Information Clearinghouse
http://naic.acf.hhs.gov/index.cfm

The adoption information branch of the United States Department of Health and Human Services. Connects professionals and the public to timely and balanced information on programs, research, legislation, and statistics on adoption.

Adoption Booksellers

Tapestry Books (www.tapestrybooks.com)
Alphabet Books (www.alphabetsoupbookstore.com)
Multicultural Kids (www.multiculturalkids.com)
Celebrate the Child (www.celebratechild.com)
AdoptionBooks.com (www.adoptionbooks.com)

Acknowledgments

Thank you to Molly Mullen Ward and the rest of our wonderful team at LifeLine Press—Beth Mottar, Lauren Lawson, John Lalor, Amanda Larsen, and Kristina Phillips—for their enthusiastic dedication to this project; to Kathryn Creedy, adoption author, for her wise and generous counsel; to Elizabeth Lyon and Polly Bowman for their invaluable editorial advice; to Robin Berenholz of Adoptions From the Heart for her early input; to Rocky Bleier, for his inspirational life; to Josh Zhong, Lily Nie, and all the extraordinary people at our adoption agency, CCAI, for our families. And most of all, thank you to Andy and Rich and to our daughters, Chloe, Audrey, and Natalie, for everything.

Index

A

Abramowitz, Caryn, x, xiv, xvi

adopted child(ren): abandonment and, 15–16, 46, 47; appearance of, xiii, 17–18, 48; birth country of, xvi, 7–8. *See also* birth country; birth parents and. *See* birth parents; bonding with new family members and, xi, 46, 49–50; boys versus girls as, 25–26; defined, 5–6; feelings of, upon learning of adoption, 39–40; girls versus boys as, 25–26; giving back, 33–34; heritage of, acknowledgment and celebration of, 50–51; introducing to others as adopted, 53–55; language and, 31–32; luck and, 55; placement of, for adoption, reasons for, 13–16, 46, 47; pre-adoption memories of, 37–38; privacy and, xv, 2, 47, 48–49; as "real" cousin, xii, 19–20; with special needs, 47; treatment of, 45–46, 55

adoption(s): adopted child's feelings upon learning about, 39–40; books about, 151; costs involved in, 29–30, 49; cross-border. *See* cross-cultural adoption(s); defined, 5–6; inappropriate use of word, 54–55; international. *See* international adoption(s); mistaken assumptions regarding, 55–56;

adoption(s)(*continued*): organizations involved with, 149–150; resources for learning more about, 149–150; transracial, xii–xiii
adoption agencies: function of, 6, 9, 29–30; payment to, 29–30, 49
Adoption Is a Family Affair (Johnston), xiv
Adoption Nation: How the Adoption Revolution Is Transforming America (Pertman), 61–62
adoption professionals: function of, 6, 9, 29–30; payment to, 29–30
Adoptive Families, 149
adoptive parents, 41–43; adopted child named by, 27–28; becoming, reasons for, 23–24, 33–34, 55–56; bonding with adopted child, xi, 46, 49–50; defined, 11; inappropriate comments regarding adoption and, xiii, 46–47, 58–59; as natural parents, 11; privacy and, xiii, 2, 23, 47; prospective, treatment of, 49–50; as "real" parents, 11, 13
AdoptiveFamilies.Com, 149
adult(s): additional information for, objectives of, 2, 3; do's and don'ts for, 41–59
Africa: single motherhood in, 57; as source of adopted children, 57. *See also individual countries*
Alexis Petrovich, 78
Aristide, Jean-Bertrand, 143
Asia: names in, 28; single motherhood in, 57; as source of adopted children, 57, 61–62. *See also individual countries*
attachment, 49–50

B

Baryshnikov, Mikhail, 81
birth country: defined, 7–8; learning about, xvi, 50–51, 61–148. *See also individual countries*
birth mothers, 47, 57–58
birth parents: adopted child named by, 27–28; adopted child's memories of, 37–38; contacting, 12, 36; criticism of, 47, 57–58; defined, 11, 13; going back with, 35–36; knowledge regarding, 12, 36; placement of child for adoption and, 13–16, 46, 47; single motherhood and, 57
Bleier, Rocky, ix–x
bonding, xi, 46, 49–50
Botero, Fernando, 136
Brando, Marlon, 81
Buddha, 96
Bulgaria, names in, 28

C

caregivers. *See* parents
Catherine the Great, 78
Central America, as source of adopted children, 62. *See also individual countries*
Chekhov, Anton, 81

The Cherry Orchard, 81
Chiang Kai-shek, 68
China: adoption process in, 47; as birth country, xi, xii, xvi, 47, 62, 65–76; culture and holidays of, 70–73; economy of, 70; food of, 73–74; geography and population of, 65–66; history and government of, 66–69; literature and other books about, 74–76; names in, 28
Chun Doo Hwan, 95
Colombia: as birth country, 133–139; culture and holidays of, 136–137; economy of, 135–136; food of, 137; geography and population of, 133–134; history and government of, 134–135; literature and other books about, 138–139; names in, 28
Columbus, Christopher, 134, 142
Confucius, 96
Coughlin, Amy, x, xiv, xvi
cross-border adoption. *See* international adoption(s)
cross-cultural adoption(s): number of, xii–xiii; reasons for, 9–10; resources for learning more about, 149–150
Cruise, Tom, 54

D

Daniel, xi–xii
DeNiro, Robert, 81
Dessalines, Jean-Jacques, 142
Duvalier, Francois, 143
Duvalier, Jean-Claude ("Baby Doc"), 143

E

English language, 31–32
Europe: names in, 28; single motherhood in, 57; as source of adopted children, 57, 61. *See also individual countries*
Evan B. Donaldson Adoption Institute, 149–150
expectant parents, treatment of, 49–50

F

Farewell My Concubine, 72
The Firebird, 81
Fodor's, 51
foster parents: adopted child named by, before adoption, 27–28; adopted child's memories of, 38; function of, 21, 22

G

Gaitan, Jorge Eliecer, 135
Gandhi, Indira, 117
Gandhi, Mohandas K., 117
Gandhi, Rajiv, 117
Germany, as birth country, 61
Gorbachev, Mikhail, 79
governmental organizations: function of, in adoption process, 6, 9, 29–30; payments to, 29–30, 49
Greece, as birth country, 61

Guatemala: as birth country, 85–91; culture and holidays of, 88–89; economy of, 88; food of, 89–90; geography and population of, 85–86; history and government of, 86–88; literature and other books about, 90–91; names in, 28

H

Hackman, Gene, 53
Haiti: as birth country, 141–148; culture and holidays of, 144–146; economy of, 144; food of, 146; geography and population of, 141–142; history and government of, 142–143; literature and other books about, 147–148
Hitler, Adolf, 77
Ho Chi Minh, 124–125
Hoffman, Dustin, 81

I

India: as birth country, 115–122; culture and holidays of, 118–120; economy of, 118; food of, 120; geography and population of, 115–116; history and government of, 116–118; literature and other books about, 121–122
Institute for Adoption Information, 150
international adoption(s): information about, 49; number of, xii–xiii; reasons for, 9–10

J

Japan, as birth country, 62
Johnston, Pat, xiv
Joint Council on International Children's Services, 150

K

Kazakhstan: as birth country, 101–106; culture and holidays of, 103–104; economy of, 102–103; food of, 104; geography and population of, 101–102; history and government of, 102; literature and other books about, 105–106
Kidman, Nicole, 54
Korea. *See also* South Korea: as birth country, 62; names in, 28

L

language, 31–32
lawyers, payments to, 29–30
Leguizamo, John, 136
Lenin, Vladimir, 78–79
Let's Go, 51
Lily, xi–xii
Lonely Planet, 51
L'Ouverture, Toussaint, 142
Love in the Time of Cholera (Marquez), 136

M

Mao Tse-tung, 68–69, 70, 71, 74
Marquez, Gabriel Garciá, 133, 136
Montoya, Juan, 136

N

names, 27–28
Napoleon, 77, 142
National Adoption Information Clearinghouse, 150
"natural parents," 11. *See also* adoptive parents; birth parents
Nehru, Jawaharlal, 117
Nureyev, Rudolph, 81
The Nutcracker Suite, 81

O

older children, additional information for, objectives of, 2, 3
One Hundred Years of Solitude (Marquez), 136
orphanage, 21–22; memories of, 37

P

Pacino, Al, 81
Paltrow, Gwyneth, 53
parents: adoptive. *See* birth parents; defined, 11–12; expectant, treatment of, 49–50. *See also* birth parents; "real," 11, 13; foster parents; "natural," 11.
Pavlova, Anna, 81
People's Republic of China. *See* China
Pertman, Adam, 61–62
Peter the Great, 78
privacy: adopted children and, xv, 2, 47, 48–49; adoptive parents and, xiii, 2, 23, 47

Q

Qu Yuan, 73

R

"real parents," 11, 13. *See also* adoptive parents; birth parents
Republic of Guatemala. *See* Guatemala
Republic of Korea. *See* South Korea
The Royal Tenenbaums, 53
Russia: as birth country, 77–84; culture and holidays of, 80–82; economy of, 80; food of, 82–83; geography and population of, 77–78; history and government of, 78–79; literature and other books about, 83–84; names in, 28

S

The Seagull, 81
Shah Jahan, 116
Shakira, 136
Shevchenko, Taras, 111
Shi Huangdi (emperor of China), 74
The Sleeping Beauty, 81
South America: names in, 28; single motherhood in, 57; as source of adopted children, 57, 62. *See also individual countries*
South Korea. *See also* Korea: as birth country, 62, 93–99; culture and holidays of, 96–97; economy of, 95–96; food of, 97; geography and population of, 93–94;

South Korea (*continued*).
history and government of, 94–95; literature and other books about, 98–99
Stalin, Joseph, 79
Stanislavsky, Konstantin, 81
Stravinsky, Igor Fyodorovich, 81
Sun Yat-sen, 68
Swan Lake, 81

T

Tchaikovsky, Pyotr Ilich, 81
transracial adoptions, xii–xiii

U

Ukraine, 79; as birth country, ix, x, 107–113; culture and holidays of, 110–111; economy of, 109–110; food of, 112; geography and population of, 107–108; history and government of, 108–109; literature and other books about, 112–113
Uncle Vanya, 81
U.S. State Department, 49, 63

V

Vietnam: as birth country, 62, 123–131; culture and holidays of, 126–128; economy of, 126; food of, 128–129; geography and population of, 123–124; history and government of, 124–126; literature and other books about, 130–131; names in, 28

W

The Wizard of Oz, 35, 36

Y

Yeltsin, Boris, 79
young child(ren): answers for, objectives of, 2; defined, xiii; questions asked by, xiii, xv–xvi, 1–40